Share Your Story

Blogging with MSN® Spaces

Katherine Murray and Michael Torres

PUBLISHED BY

Microsoft Press
A Division of Microsoft Corporation
One Microsoft Way
Redmond, Washington 98052-6399

Library of Congress Control Number 2005934151

Printed and bound in the United States of America.

1 2 3 4 5 6 7 8 9   QWT   0 9 8 7 6 5

Distributed in Canada by H.B. Fenn and Company Ltd.

A CIP catalogue record for this book is available from the British Library.

Microsoft Press books are available through booksellers and distributors worldwide. For further information about international editions, contact your local Microsoft Corporation office or contact Microsoft Press International directly at fax (425) 936-7329. Visit our Web site at www.microsoft.com/learning/. Send comments to *mspinput@microsoft.com*.

Microsoft, Hotmail, MSN, Windows, and Windows Media are either registered trademarks or trademarks of Microsoft Corporation in the United States and/or other countries.

The example companies, organizations, products, domain names, e-mail addresses, logos, people, places, and events depicted herein are fictitious. No association with any real company, organization, product, domain name, e-mail address, logo, person, place, or event is intended or should be inferred.

This book expresses the author's views and opinions. The information contained in this book is provided without any express, statutory, or implied warranties. Neither the authors, Microsoft Corporation, nor its resellers or distributors will be held liable for any damages caused or alleged to be caused either directly or indirectly by this book.

Acquisitions Editors: Juliana Aldous-Atkins, Duane Draper
Project Editor: Valerie Woolley
Production and Editorial Services: Happenstance Type-O-Rama

Photograph on pages 35 and 118 by Frank Huster

Body Part No. X11-50521

To everybody with a story to tell, a passion to share, a question to ask, or an opinion to offer— come share your story with us on MSN Spaces!

CONTENTS AT A GLANCE

CONTENTS

Share Your Story: Blogging with MSN Spaces

Home | Profile | Blog | Photos | Lists | Friends

Profile

Mike Torres

Credits and Thanks

This book showcases the skill and effort of many people. Special thanks to these talented people:

Valerie, Sandra, and Juliana at Microsoft Press

Laurie, Guy, Kim, and Chris at Happenstance

Everyone on the MSN Spaces team

Claudette Moore at Moore Literary Agency

Blog

Welcome!

Hello! And welcome to our space! The book that you hold in your hands is the result of months of discovery, fun, collaboration, and well, yes, effort on the part of many people. We wrote this book during an exciting time and were able to be part of the process as MSN Spaces was going through its second major development cycle. As a result, we had the advantage of working with the already popular MSN Spaces interface while at the same time building our examples on the latest and greatest versions of MSN Spaces still in development. You'll find ideas, tips, and interviews in here that you won't be able to find in any other book on MSN Spaces. The only wrinkle is that some of the figures you see in this book may be slightly different from what you'll see on your monitor today. As this book was going to press, exciting new features in photos, friends, and spaces search were just about to be released to the public. We tried to capture all of the new look for you, but in the fast-moving world of online technology, things begin changing as soon as they're born!

Some of the special features you'll find in *Share Your Story: Blogging with MSN Spaces* include the following:

- All the how-tos for creating and setting up your space
- Ideas for creating a network of friends and family
- Suggestions for adding great lists to your space
- Tips for uploading, editing, and displaying your photos online
- MSN Spaces backstory interviews with program managers and developers
- Tips and tricks for personalizing and improving your space
- Special undocumented PowerToy techniques

We hope you'll enjoy the time you spend here in our 3D book space and that you'll be inspired to try your hand at creating and sharing your own stories. Our shared book space (where you'll be able to find tips and stories about MSN Spaces as time goes on) is http://spaces.msn.com/msnspacesbook: stop by and say hello sometime!

All the best,

Kathy and Mike

Add a comment
8:48 AM | Permalink | Trackbacks (0) | Blog it

Photo album

Working ▽   Slideshow ▽

▶   ■ |◀   ▶|

Description | Katherine Murray | Comments (0)

Special Thanks

[Kathy] THANKS! to Mike Torres for being a great coauthor and bringing expertise, ability, and humor. Let's do it again soon. :)

[Mike] Special thanks to my wife, Melinda, for being by my side through this process and encouraging me to do this. And to my mother, father, and sister, Karen, for all of their help over the years and for not disowning me for never calling them back!

[Mike] Special thanks to Kathy for being one of the most optimistic people I know and for all the great advice on my first book. It couldn't have been better!

Introducing MSN Spaces

CHAPTER 1

Hello! Welcome to a whole new way to share your favorite things—stories, photos, music, movies, and more—with family and friends, new and old. MSN Spaces is more than just an easy-to-use blogging tool; it's a complete creative online communications world that enables you to write your stories (if words are your thing), post your pictures (if you want to show *and* tell), and create lists of your favorites (sites, movies, books, music, or people). And best of all, you get to be part of a vibrant, growing community—sharing stories, interests, and ideas with people all over the world.

With MSN Spaces, you get to be part of a vibrant, growing community—sharing stories, interests, and ideas with people all over the world.

And while you're on your space sharing who you are and what you know, you can work easily with MSN Hotmail, MSN Messenger, and other Microsoft tools such as MSN Search Toolbar and MSN Screen Saver. Expressing yourself isn't only fun; it's also convenient, fast, and easy. Tap into that creative spirit. It's your turn to share what you have to say—by blogging, uploading photos, creating lists, sending e-mail, using instant messaging, and more. And it's all in one convenient, easy-to-use place. *Your* space.

This chapter gives you a bird's-eye view of MSN Spaces and helps you begin thinking about how you'll use your own space. Here you'll find out about the benefits of MSN Spaces, learn how you can be part of the community, and get a sense of the fast-moving history of blogging so you can see where you fit into the larger scheme of personal publishing. Ready to get started? Let's begin.

Blogging Basics

When you first learned about MSN Spaces, you may have heard it called a *blogging tool*, but it's really much more than that. Blogging is a personal publishing phenomenon that in recent years has grown to the size of a movement, enabling individuals to share their stories, ideas, commentary, and more on the Web, where others can read and respond to their writing. Blogging abounds on the Web, offering colorful personal perspectives on all sorts of topics—from technology to culture to politics and more. People blog for pleasure—to share their stories with the world—and with purpose (to comment on and contribute to the ongoing conversation about the media, government, technology, and more). In fact, blogging has become such a force in its own right that it can sway public opinion, highlight stories that missed the mainstream media, and create a call for investigation when others seem to be looking the other way. Adults who once relied primarily on network news are increasingly turning to their favorite bloggers (and to Jon Stewart on Comedy Central!) to get news and commentary on the events of the day.

A QUICK BLOG HISTORY

As early as the 1980s, people were connecting on the Internet. Granted, it was a bit like the dinosaur age, as far as computers go. But through e-mail lists, discussion boards, and some early chat rooms, users were able to use the Web to share real information in (sometimes) real time. It was a movement with so much energy that it was sure to mushroom quickly.

The arrival of tools that made Web publishing available to the masses brought the first real glimmer of blogging potential to the scene. Now people who were brave enough to learn the code and master the tools could publish their own thoughts, images, and creations to the Web. Soon we figured out how to link to other pages, and still more, and then more. In a real sense, the Web became just that—a world-wide web.

> For an interesting Wikipedia article on the history and nature of blogging, surf to http://en.wikipedia.org/wiki/Weblog.
>
> TIP

As more people started publishing personal Web pages, companies developed services to help them do it more easily. You may have heard of the free blogging service Blogger; TypePad and LiveJournal are two other popular blogging sites. These sites help users get their thoughts and images up on the Web, also providing an easy way for users to archive their writings in an accessible format. And interest continued to grow.

At the same time blogging was developing from personal Web publishing, a new wave was forming on the Web. This wave was about building community—a myriad of "friend" sites were linked and maintained through the growing blogging audience.

Utilities such as Blogroll.com (a free utility that enables bloggers to display links to all their favorite blogs) helped blogging become a social networking tool. Friend sites such as Friendster, MySpace, and Flickr focused on offering users a social connection rather than touting their blog features. And people—especially college students and young adults—swarmed to the sites, adding friends and friends of friends and doing both amazing and strange things on their sites.

Each of these sites placed a bigger emphasis on the connecting aspect of the Web, encouraging people to create a profile, invite their friends, upload photos, and more. Popular especially among young adults and older teens, these sites enabled members to cultivate their connections, continually enlarging their social network through a controlled but far-reaching web of interconnections.

Another swell of interest occurred because of the excitement and accessibility of digital photography. When good digital cameras became more affordable, we started bringing our many megabytes of digital images to the Web for storing, distributing, and printing. And new sites are being developed all the time that enable users to share their photos (and some work better than others).

So, three major threads of blossoming Web interest came together to create the possibilities we have today—publishing personal content online, building communities with those we enjoy and admire, and posting and sharing our favorite photos. We can show and tell the stories of our lives in a real way, in and among a community of people who are sharing what's most important to them in the course of a day.

ENTER MSN SPACES: SOMETHING FOR EVERYONE

In MSN Spaces, you get the best of all possible worlds—easy-to-use blogging features; simple but powerful photo organizing, editing, and displaying options; and the networking potential you need to build your own community and interact with friends and family. Add to that the instant connection possibilities through MSN Hotmail and MSN Messenger, and you've got a Web full of possibilities for expressing yourself and keeping in touch. The next section introduces you to some of the specific benefits MSN Spaces offers.

LEARNING THE MSN SPACES LINGO

Before we get too far into the chapter, we'll take a minute to define some terms. Here are some of the terms you'll see throughout this book:

Space   This is your Web page in MSN Spaces. You can post text, photos, and links on your space; link to other spaces; add audio and video; and customize the look of your space.

List   A list in MSN Spaces enables you to share your favorite books, music, movies, friends' spaces, tricks, and more. You can create custom lists to show off your own interests.

Photo album   A photo album displays photos you upload to MSN Spaces by presenting them in a continually running slide show. You can change the size of photo albums and create as many different photos albums as you'd like.

Blog entry   A blog entry is the text you enter on your space. Different from a list entry, a blog entry is typically a block of text relating a story, a thought, a poem, or something about your day and usually includes a heading and a date. You can add photos to your blog entry to help visitors get a better sense of what you're describing.

Profile   Your space profile tells your visitors a little about you. You can customize your profile to show as much or as little about you as you'd like. Options include displaying your photo, revealing your name and age, showing where you live, and cataloging your hobbies and interests.

The Perks of MSN Spaces

If you've spent any time exploring other blogging services, you'll immediately notice the ways in which MSN Spaces is different from the rest. Here are the pleasant surprises you'll find as you create your space:

- You never have to type a single Hypertext Markup Language (HTML) tag to publish your blog entry.

- You can create your space and add content in ten minutes or less.

- You can easily upload and share music lists, photos, video clips, and more.

- You have a huge amount of storage for your photos.

- You feel part of a worldwide community.

- You can syndicate your updates (or get updates from your favorite spaces automatically).

- You can use MSN Spaces and MSN Messenger, and even MSN Hotmail, seamlessly together to cover all your bases for online communication.

NO CODING REQUIRED

The MSN Spaces blogging feature includes all the tools you need to create blog entries that look just the way you want them to look—no coding necessary. When you click Add Entry in the Blog module (more about this in Chapter 4, "Adding and Editing Blog Entries"), the window that is displayed gives you everything you need to write, format, and publish your thoughts (see Figure 1-1).

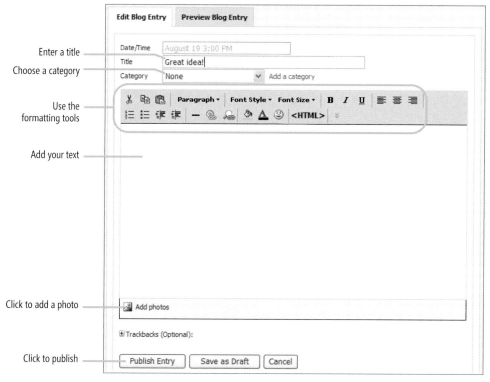

Figure 1-1: The blogging window gives you all the tools you need for entering, formatting, and publishing your entry.

Just because you don't *have* to use HTML doesn't mean your options are limited. If you're comfortable with coding and want to use HTML to add special items or formatting, you can click HTML Mode in the Edit Blog Entry window and enter your text the good, old-fashioned, hand-coded way.

EXPRESS YOURSELF, YOUR WAY—FAST!

As soon as you create your space, you'll realize that posting is simple. MSN Spaces is set up so that you can tell or show your stories in whatever way is easiest for you. Maybe you think in lists (see Figure 1-2)—*What did I do today? Who did I see? What was the most fun?* Or maybe you think in images (see Figure 1-3)—*Gosh, I have that great photo of Val at the beach. I should put that up.* Or maybe you think in stories— *I should write about that time Herb got stuck trying to climb into the locked car through the sunroof!* (A friendly tip: you might want to ask Herb whether that's OK first!) MSN Spaces makes it easy for you to create lists, upload photos, or write and post stories—whatever your style, MSN Spaces supports it. In ten minutes, you could have some real content up on the Web. No, it's not an exaggeration. Try it and see!

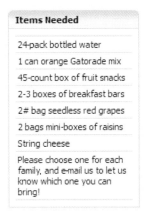

Figure 1-2 (left): If you're a list maker, you'll feel right at home with MSN Spaces.

Figure 1-3 (right): Create photo albums of your favorite images, and invite your friends to view and comment on your photos.

MSN Spaces also includes mobile features that make it easy for you to post photos and add blog entries while you're away from home. See Chapter 4, "Adding and Editing Blog Entries," for more about mobile posting.

TIP

HUGE PHOTO STORAGE SPACE

Across the Web, photo-sharing sites have become hugely popular. We want to be able to store our photos, share them with others, and order them online with just a few clicks of the mouse. Now, in MSN Spaces, you can create multiple photo albums to store photos related to different events, people, places, and themes. And you start with room for thousands of your photos—that's a *lot* of room to fill. The photos in the photo album you select display on your space in a slide-show format, adding movement and interest to your page (and keeping your visitors engaged).

And creating a photo album is easy. You simply click Edit Your Space and then click Create Photo Album. In the window that appears, you enter a name for the album, click the Add Photos link, choose the photos you want, and click Save and Close (see Figure 1-4). That's it!

 TIP
Chapter 5, "Sharing Your Photos," is all about the visuals. Explore that chapter to learn how to edit, upload, view, and arrange your photos in MSN Spaces.

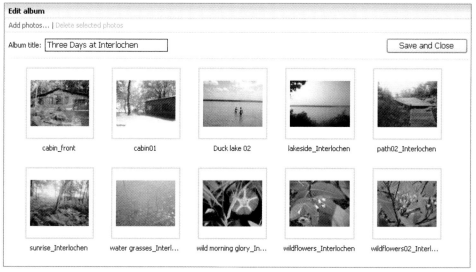

Figure 1-4: Uploading and working with your photos is simple in MSN Spaces—and you have lots of storage space, so you can include all the photos you want to share.

MORE THAN WORDS

Although other blogging services tend to be heavy on text features (meaning they give you the tools you need to write, edit, format, and post blog entries), MSN Spaces improves the ease with which you can include music, photos, and video on your space. Communicating isn't a two-dimensional act anymore with one person writing and another one reading. Now you can hear, see, watch, and absorb what space creators want to share with you. Figure 1-5 shows the new Windows Media Player PowerToy that was released in August 2005.

Figure 1-5: You can add music and video with the new PowerToys available for MSN Spaces.

Text is important in MSN Spaces, but the point is that now you have the choice and the power to communicate your stories in the way that suits you best—in words, pictures, lists, video, or music. You have many options for making your stories come alive. Experiment with the photo and music features of MSN Spaces, and—who knows?—maybe soon, you'll be creating your own podcasts.

> **NOTE** PowerToys are undocumented features, so they require a little bit of an adventurous spirit—but they aren't hard to use, and they add appeal to your space. For more about using PowerToys on your space, see Chapter 7, "Your Space, Your Way."

> **TIP** What's a podcast? Similar to an on-demand audio or video webcast, a podcast enables you to create a customized broadcast that you make available on your space. Visitors to your space can then download the broadcast to their MP3 players and listen to it on the go.

BE PART OF A WORLDWIDE COMMUNITY

MSN Spaces adds the aspect of community to blogging in a way that enables blog-gers to do what they do best—share ideas, thoughts, opinions, and suggestions—in a huge, diverse, ongoing, multifaceted conversation. With MSN Spaces, you see the Updated Spaces list just about everywhere you go, enabling you to click a link and see who has just updated their space with new information. And your space will be displayed on the Updated Spaces list as well, which makes your space visible and available to millions of other MSN Spaces users. When you find a space you like, you can add the space to your Favorites list (or create a list to display your favorite spaces); and others can do the same for you. The community grows and spreads as new people discover your space and use trackbacks and comments to play off your thoughts and interests.

And what's more, you can get people actively engaged on your space by inviting them to add comments on your photos and blog entries (and by responding to them when they do). And while you're doing all that networking, you can put some energy into building your Friends list so that you can keep track of all your favorite people online and keep in touch by stopping by their spaces regularly.

Are you getting a sense of the big picture? You're part of a worldwide conversation that has already begun—in text and pictures—all over the Web. And it's available to you in your own space on MSN Spaces.

SYNDICATE YOUR SPACE

Once you get the hang of posting to your space, you may find it addicting. Getting positive feedback from others, establishing new connections, and watching the num-ber of site visits rise really helps you build momentum on your space. It's especially fun to see users come back time and time again to see what you're posting, to notice what's new, and to link to their own spaces for more discussion.

MSN Spaces includes a Really Simple Syndication (RSS) feed capability, which means you can *syndicate* (or distribute by subscription) the content of your space to people who are interested in receiving it. This helps you build your audience and send infor-mation to people who really want it. For more about syndicating your space, see Appendix A, "RSS Q&A: Interview with an RSS Aficionado."

WHERE IN THE WORLD ARE PEOPLE USING SPACES?

Since its launch, MSN Spaces has rapidly gained popularity all over the world. Tens of millions of MSN Spaces users are now busy blogging, sharing photos, and creating community in the following countries, among others:

United States	Russia
China	Israel
Canada	Antarctica
Brazil	Tuvalu
United Kingdom	Vatican City

ALL DOORS LEAD TO (AND FROM) MSN SPACES

One of the striking features of working with MSN Spaces as an online blogging service is that it has such wide reach that other popular programs work seamlessly with it. For example, once you create a space, you can move directly to that space from MSN Messenger (see Figure 1-6). When your name appears in someone else's MSN Messenger window, your name will have a special gleam if you've updated your space last, which is a visual cue to people that they need to visit your space. (See Chapter 8, "Sharing Spaces and Creating Community," for more information.)

> The partnership among MSN Messenger, MSN Spaces, and MSN Hotmail is continuing to grow, bringing greater flexibility and easier access to contacts for MSN Spaces users. Check out Chapter 9, "Extending Your Spaces Experience," for ideas on how to use these three programs together.

TIP

USING MSN SPACES POWERTOYS!

Because MSN Spaces is so easy to learn and has great appeal, users can figure out the basics of the program quickly—and then they're ready for more! In late summer of 2005, the MSN Spaces development team released a set of MSN Spaces PowerToys that enable MSN Spaces users to add music and video to spaces, customize the look and feel of spaces, and add a special HTML "sandbox" feature that lets user try out their favorite Web gadgets. To find out more about the MSN Spaces PowerToys and other up-to-date MSN Spaces happenings, browse to the team's space at http://spaces.msn.com/members/thespacecraft/.

Figure 1-6: Others can move from their MSN Messenger windows to your space with a single click of the mouse.

Finding Spaces You Like

This section of the chapter gives you a guided tour through MSN Spaces. You won't actually learn how to sign up and start your own space here (you'll do that in Chapter 2, "Getting a Space of Your Own"), but you'll get a tour of features and ideas you may want to try in your own space. Consider it a kind of "homes-of-the-stars" tour, without the map...or the bus!

Start by going to the MSN Spaces home page, available at http://spaces.msn.com. In the lower-right corner on the right side of the page, you'll find the Updated Spaces list (see Figure 1-7). This includes links to spaces that have been updated in the last several minutes. Click one of the links that looks interesting to you...and you're on your way! Enjoy reading and navigating to other spaces. Not all MSN Spaces users display the Updated Spaces list on their sites, but you can always return to the MSN Spaces home page and click another space to read.

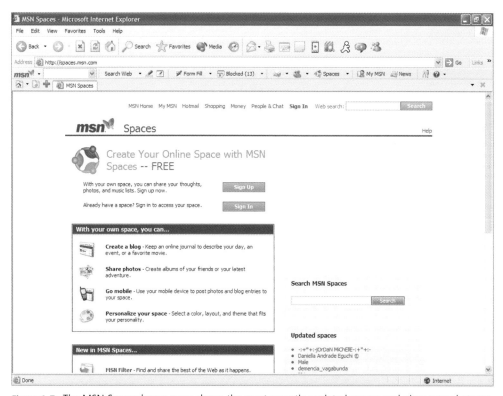

Figure 1-7: The MSN Spaces home page shows the most recently updated spaces and gives you what you need to sign up for a space.

SEARCHING FOR SPECIFIC TOPICS

If you don't see any spaces you want to view on the MSN Spaces home page, click More at the bottom of the Updated Spaces list. A full page of updated spaces will display so that you can find one you want to view.

If you want to search for other spaces that mention a topic particularly close to your heart (such as Newfoundlands), click Search (see Figure 1-8). The list is revised to show the spaces that include at least one reference to the word or phrase you entered.

As you're looking at other spaces, notice the features you like—and the features you don't. What colors appeal to you? Which fonts are just *too much*? Where do you want to stay and read? What backgrounds really work well with the color of the text? Noticing what you like about other spaces will help you make some decisions when designing your own.

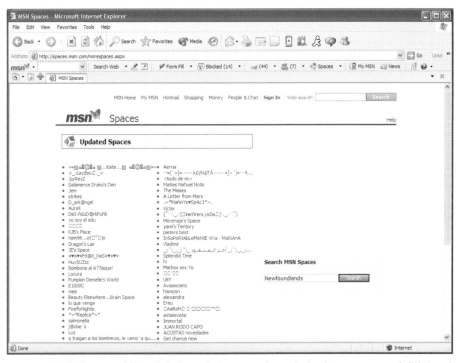

Figure 1-8: To find spaces of like-minded people, just enter the topic that interests you, and click Search.

RECEIVING SYNDICATED CONTENT

MSN Spaces has another feature that enables members to syndicate their spaces so that visitors can sign up to get updates delivered to them. You'll find out more about this RSS feature in Appendix A, "RSS Q&A: Interview with an RSS Aficionado."

SAVING YOUR FAVORITE SPACES

Enjoy browsing the spaces! When you find spaces you particularly like, you can save them in your Favorites folder by following these steps:

1. Click the Favorites tool in your Internet Explorer toolbar.

2. In the Favorites panel, click Add. The Add Favorite dialog box appears (see Figure 1-9).

3. Choose the folder in which you want to store the space; then click OK.

    Now you can return to that space whenever you choose by clicking the Favorites tool in the IE toolbar, navigating to the folder in which you saved the space's URL, and clicking the space address.

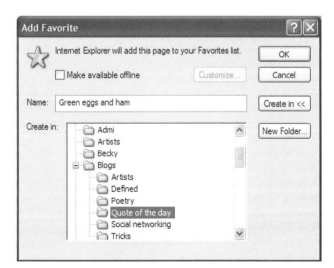

Figure 1-9: When you find a space you like, add it to your Favorites list.

MSN SPACES BACKSTORY: THE ORIGIN OF MSN SPACES

Michael Connolly, a product unit manager at MSN Spaces (http://spaces.msn.com/ emcee/), has this to say about the origins of MSN Spaces:

Q: Where did the idea of MSN Spaces come from?

A: We started with a small group of people, about four, who put together some ideas in a little mocked-up demo on what we could do in the area of "sharing." This was in the fall of 2003. That demo looked really good, so we got permission to pull a bunch of people from existing teams and just focus on prototyping on the concept.

Q: What was involved in putting together the first beta of MSN Spaces?

A: The prototyping was fun, but it was just prototyping. After we had a routine visit with one of our colleagues in our Japan office around January 2004, we thought there was a real opportunity in the Japanese market to get a simple blogging application out there that had a mobile interface. We would be able to ship a beta and learn how people would use our stuff, and the Japan team would get a public beta that they could showcase to their users.

The problem was that we absolutely needed a mobile interface for it to be successful in Japan, and we didn't have anyone on the team who knew how to create a site for Japanese phones. Not to go into the gory details, but those phones are not like the phones you find here in the U.S.

We shipped the Japan beta in the summer of 2004. We learned a lot about how to scale our site and how to work on both a mobile interface and the normal PC site at the same time, making both great.

Q: How did people respond to the beta of MSN Spaces?

A: The beta was our real rallying cry. Once we had that shipped, we kept going full steam, adding a lot more focus on photo sharing, as well as our "gleam" design with MSN Messenger.

We were considered an experiment internally, but we had only one request of other teams. We needed to get the gleam into MSN Messenger. We focused on making it really easy to implement on their side, and they did us a big favor and hooked it up for us.

The rest is history. We shipped worldwide on December 2nd, 2004.

Q: What's next for the MSN Spaces team?

A: We continue to work every day to make Spaces deeper and more interesting for our millions of users. But, it's always important to keep shipping and learning. So, even with a big secret release under development, we managed to continue to sneak out new features every now and then. And there are always creative ideas to try—so keep your eyes open!

Getting a Space of Your Own

CHAPTER 2

Now that you've seen all the possibilities MSN Spaces offers, are you ready to dive in and create your own space? Whether your goal is to create photo albums to show family members, get your friends together online, or blog your experiences to share with the world, your first step involves setting up your MSN Spaces account and creating your space. And what's more—MSN Spaces gives you a variety of ways to express yourself. You can set up and access your space using your computer or your mobile phone (yes, you read that right!), and you can get to MSN Spaces from links in MSN Messenger, MSN Music, the MSN toolbar, and other online partners.

All roads lead to MSN Spaces! You can even set up your space on a mobile phone.

Signing Up for MSN Spaces

The first step in getting your own space involves signing up for a Microsoft Passport Network account. A Passport account is used by various Microsoft sites for authentication—it verifies that you are who you say you are and enables you to simplify the whole sign-in process whenever you log in to any Microsoft site. You just enter your username and password once, and the information is stored on your computer and entered for you whenever you access another Passport-enabled site. It's a quick way to access your information without having to remember and retype it repeatedly.

NOTE — If you already have an MSN Hotmail account, you already have a Microsoft Passport, so you can simply enter your Hotmail address to sign in.

The Passport account is free and takes only a couple of minutes to complete. Here are the steps:

1. Go to the MSN Spaces home page at http://spaces.msn.com, and click Sign Up (see Figure 2-1). This starts the Passport process.

2. In the next window, click Sign Up again (see Figure 2-2).

    Why twice? Just in case the first click was a mistake and you meant to click Sign In instead of Sign Up, you have the option of entering your sign-in info in the panel to the left and signing into MSN Spaces. But for our purposes, because you're creating a new account, you need to click Sign Up a second time.

Figure 2-1: If you don't have a Microsoft Passport Network or MSN Hotmail account, you need to sign up for one to get your space.

Figure 2-2: Click Sign Up to begin the process of creating your own space.

③ The Passport process will ask you a series of simple questions, including the following:

- Do you have an e-mail address? (You can use an existing e-mail address or create a new MSN Hotmail account.)

- What do you want to use as a password? (The program will give you suggestions for creating a strong password—such as mixing upper- and lowercase letters and including numbers and symbols—and show the strength of your entry proposed password in the Password Strength bar.)

- What is your password response question (for the inevitable time when you go to enter your password and zone out)?

- What are the characters you see in the mystery box? (This is used to determine that you're in fact a breathing, living person and not a computer autobot with the evil intent of spamming the Web into oblivion.)

  Answer these questions to the best of your ability (there's no test later), and—just to be safe—write down the e-mail address you used and the password you selected. (You might also want to make a note of the password question you selected, too.) When you click Continue, you're asked to provide some pretty painless information about yourself.

④ Click Continue again, then type your e-mail address in the box, and click Accept.

That's it! All in under five minutes.

Next you'll see a screen telling you that you've created your Passport account. Congratulations! And now you can start the fun part....

Naming and Creating Your Space

The steps involved in creating your own space are really exciting because you get to focus on you: choose just the right name for your space, select the name for your Web address, and then begin creating the space you want, your way. As you create your space, you'll be able to make choices about the design, theme, colors, and Web parts that will let you say what you want to say and show what you want to show.

This part of the process begins with the Create Your Space page (see Figure 2-3). (You're taken to this page automatically after you create a Passport account using the steps outlined previously.) The first choice is a fun one: what do you want to call your space? You probably have lots of creative ideas—be sure to come up with something uniquely you. You could use a favorite phrase from your favorite movie, a family quote, a name, an image—or something entirely random! The choice is yours.

Here are the steps you need to follow:

1. Type your title in the first line.

2. Enter a shortened version of the title for the URL in step 2, and click the Check Availability button.

This will tell you whether that Web address is already in use. If the address is in use, MSN Spaces will prompt you to enter another name. Continue entering names until you come up with one that isn't in use.

③ Click the down arrow, and choose your time zone from the list.

④ Click the Service Agreement link, and review the MSN Spaces usage terms; then click the checkbox to accept the agreement.

⑤ Click Create Your Space.

A Congratulations page lets you know you've completed the process and tells you about MSN Spaces permissions. You can choose different permission settings to control who gets to see and add comments to your space (you'll learn more about these settings in the "Setting Permissions" section). For now, click Go To Your Space to get your first glimpse of your new space.

The type of permission enabled on your space by default depends on your locale in the Microsoft Passport Network. In most areas, the default permission setting is Public, but in some places, spaces are set by default to MSN Messenger.

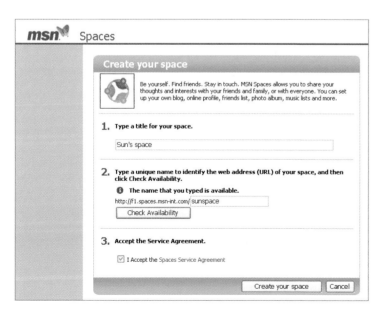

Figure 2-3: Enter a title for your space, and check the availability of your member name.

ON THE GO? SET UP MOBILE MSN SPACES

Did you know you can sign up for your own space using your mobile phone? Simply use your Web access setting to go to http://spaces.msn.com, and MSN Spaces will offer you a text menu for creating your space (or accessing an existing one). Click Sign In, and then click to sign up for a new Passport account (or enter your user ID and password). That gets you started. Amazing!

NOTE
If for some reason the page doesn't load correctly on your model of cell phone (all cell phones aren't created equal!), navigate to http://mobile.spaces.msn.com to access the Sign In option.

Introducing Your Home Space

If you've done any browsing around other spaces, you already know that you'll have a lot of work to do to make this new space look like home (see Figure 2-4). But don't be discouraged—you'd be surprised how quickly it begins to look great. Soon you'll be choosing new colors, arranging the Web parts, adding a profile, and posting pho- tos and text—and then it will have all the comfort of a real home space.

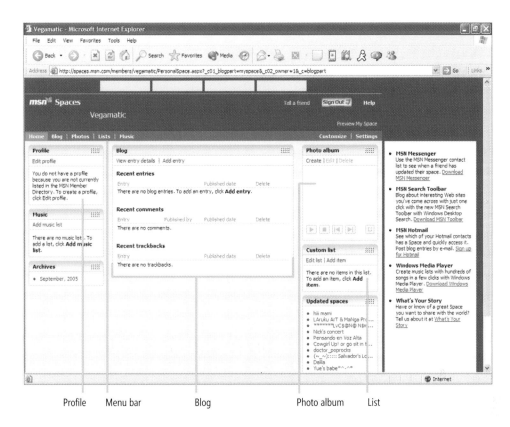

Profile   Menu bar   Blog   Photo album   List

Figure 2-4: You have a lot to do to make *this* look like home!

Before you start decorating, however, take a moment to look around the space. This list calls your attention to some key items on your space you may want to return to later:

Edit mode   Whenever you sign in to your space, it is displayed in Edit mode. You'll know this is Edit mode when you see the small options listed under the list titles. For example, when your space is displayed in Edit mode, the photo album shows Create | Edit | Delete beneath the title bar. You'll use Edit mode to make changes to your space, add information, upload photos, and more. To change to Preview mode (which is the way people visiting your space will see it), click Preview My Space in the upper-right corner of the space.

Tabs The tabs at the top of the space give you a variety of ways to work with and customize your space.

Profile area The Profile area enables you to enter and update information about yourself and your interests.

Editable lists A variety of lists are already created for you: you can add info to the music list or create custom lists with your own information. (See Chapter 6, "Sharing Lists of Songs, Books, and More," for the details on adding list information to your space.)

Noneditable lists Two lists—Archives and Updated Spaces—can't be updated and are displayed by default, but you can hide them if you want to do so.

Photo album The photo album enables you to post, organize, and share your favorite photos.

Chapter 3, "Describing Yourself," walks you through the process of setting up your profile so you can introduce yourself to the world (or at least to your space mates).

Thinking through Space Settings

Some people just can't wait to put everything they possibly can up on their space—and others are more reserved. Some people want to be able to publish photos and blog entries from their mobile phones (known as *moblogging* for "mobile blogging"); others just want to figure out the basics of space making first.

No matter what your interests and preferences, MSN Spaces gives you a whole variety of settings you can use to set up your space your way. If your space is currently in Preview mode, start by clicking Edit Your Space to turn on Edit mode; then click Settings (on the right side of the MSN Spaces window). New selections appear across the top of the space's area. Each of these items gives you a different group of settings to work with in your space: Space Settings, Blog Settings, Permissions, E-mail Publishing, Storage, Statistics, and Communications Preferences.

WHAT DOES IT MEAN TO SYNDICATE YOUR SPACE?

Similar to a popular television show that is in syndication or a favorite newspaper column that is syndicated nationwide, syndicating your space means you're able to distribute the content you add (photos and text) so that people interested in receiving it get it automatically. This happens seamlessly—and all you need to do is click the Syndicate checkbox on the Space Settings tab! Your viewers will need to have an RSS reader to read the syndicated information, but free RSS readers are available from a number of sites. (Check out http://www.start.com for a cool, new Web-based RSS reader.)

To get the lowdown on RSS and understand how you can receive syndicated content from your favorite spaces, see Appendix A, "RSS Q&A: Interview with an RSS Aficionado."

CHOOSING YOUR SPACE SETTINGS

Go to Space Settings when you want to change some of the big-picture elements of your space. For example, if you want to change the title or add a subtitle, syndicate your space so others can receive your updates automatically, or even delete your space, you do it on the Space Settings tab. Click Save after you enter your selections.

THE BASICS OF BLOG SETTINGS

Yes, the word *blog* is strange if you're not familiar with it. But bear with us—by the time you finish Chapter 4, "Adding and Editing Blog Entries," you'll know all about blogging. Put simply, a *blog entry* is like a journal entry that you post on your space. You might write an entry about a family outing, a new game you're trying, or an experience with a loved one, or you might add a poem, a thought, or a quote.

When you click the Blog Settings tab, several settings appear that enable you to choose how many posts you display on your MSN Spaces home page. You can also choose whether you want the blog entries arranged by title or by date. (If you don't update your blog regularly, you might want to downplay the date by choosing the Show Date in Footer option.) Additionally, you can choose whether you want to allow comments and trackbacks (more on these in a bit). Finally, you can let MSN Spaces know whether you want ping servers to be notified when you update your space (ping servers let sites know when your space has been updated, which is a really great way to increase your space's visibility), and you can enter the categories you want to use to help you organize and sort your blog entries.

TIP

Comments and trackbacks are two features that can help raise the visibility of your space. If you want to increase the readership of your space and get a conversation going with your viewers, be sure to click the Allow Comments checkbox on the Blog Settings tab. Trackbacks enable you to refer to other blogs (and they can refer to you) so you can increase the number of links connected with your site. MSN Spaces enables you to set three levels of trackbacks—you can allow trackbacks from all sites, allow trackbacks from only other MSN Spaces, and completely disable trackbacks.

SETTING PERMISSIONS

Setting the permissions you want for your space is an important part of the setup process. MSN Spaces enables you to choose different levels of permissions (see Figure 2-5). If you want anyone and everyone to see your space (the more, the better!), leave your space set to Public. If you want to limit the number of people who can view your space to only those who are on your MSN Messenger list, click the Messenger Allow List permission level. If you want to allow the friends you add in your Friends list, plus their friends, you can choose Friends of Friends & Messenger. Click Save to activate the new permission setting.

PUBLISHING BY E-MAIL

Who says you have to be tied to a computer in order to express yourself on MSN Spaces? If you have a mobile phone with e-mail capability, you can post blog entries to your space from anyplace you can get a signal. Traveling in Hong Kong? Send your stories (and your photos, if you have a camera phone) to MSN Spaces in real time and update your space from another continent!

Turn on e-mail publishing by clicking the checkbox and entering the e-mail address from which you'll be sending your posts (see Figure 2-6). (Chances are that your cell phone's e-mail address will be your cell phone number combined with a special word from your provider. Contact your service provider for specifics.) Choose a secret word (which becomes part of the e-mail address you use to post to your space), and let MSN Spaces know whether you want to save the received messages as drafts or post them directly to your site.

> For best results, start out with the Save As Draft option selected until you have used e-mail publishing a few times and are certain your posts are formatted the way you want them to look. Some phone services may produce messages that require a bit more formatting before they're ready to publish.
>
> TIP

Finally, copy the e-mail address MSN Spaces gives you and add it to the address book you use on your mobile phone. You'll send the multimedia messages (including the photos) to that address, and MSN Spaces will take care of the rest. (For more about mobile blogging, see Chapter 4, "Adding and Editing Blog Entries.")

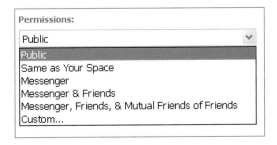

Figure 2-5: You can choose from among various permission levels to give others access to your space.

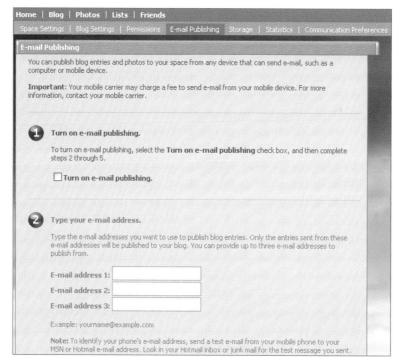

Figure 2-6: Turn on e-mail publishing to be able to post to your space from your mobile phone or e-mail.

MANAGING YOUR STORAGE SPACE

At first this may not mean much to you, but once you get in the swing of adding photos to your space, you'll use the Storage tab to delete the photos you no longer need. Figure 2-7 shows a storage space with several photos; to delete the extras, simply click the checkboxes of the ones you want to remove, and click the Delete button at the bottom of the page.

SEEING WHO'S VISITING YOUR SITE

The next tab in the Settings area of your space gives you a peek into some fascinating information—who is visiting your site? The Statistics tab shows you how many people have been to your site since you created it and lists the number of visits for

the current week and the current day. What's more, a list of hits shows you the referring Web addresses of people who are coming to your space. This is great information to have, especially if you want to increase the readership of your space. (See
Chapter 8, "Connecting Spaces and Creating Community," for more information on
statistics.)

If you see a link on the Statistics tab that lets you know someone has come to
your space through a search engine such as MSN Search or Google, click the
link to see what the person was searching for on that site. This gives you a clue
about what people are finding most interesting on your space—and that's
helpful because you can always publish more of it!

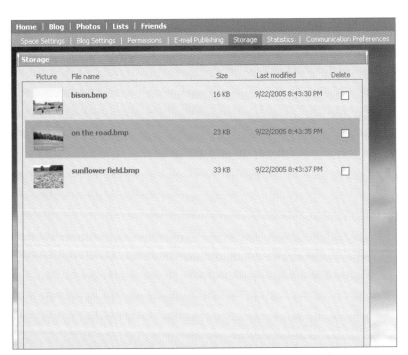

Figure 2-7: Use the Storage tab to remove photos you no longer need.

COMMUNICATING YOUR WAY

The Communication Preferences tab in your MSN Spaces settings enables you to specify what you want to be invited to and by whom (see Figure 2-8). You can let MSN Spaces know who you want to receive MSN Messenger invitations from; additionally, you can specify those you want to invite to your space or establish live contact with. You'll use the Communication Preferences tab to further control the way in which you reach out to and communicate with others.

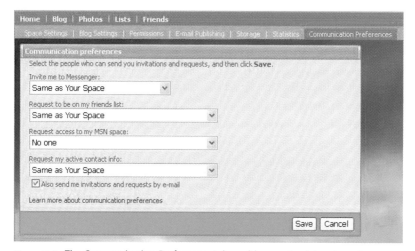

Figure 2-8: The Communication Preferences tab enables you to determine who you have contact with in various ways.

Customizing Your Space

Now for the really fun part. MSN Spaces is all about expressing yourself your way, so you have plenty of ways to make your space uniquely yours. You can choose from dozens of themes with vibrant colors and backgrounds designs—and even better, you can change the theme as often as you like. You can add new lists to your page, hide ones are already there, and choose different layouts to totally organize your space.

To start the process, make sure your space is in Edit mode, and click Customize (to the left of the Settings options). Four new options appear at the top of the MSN Spaces window: Themes, Modules, Layout, and Background.

Choosing Your Theme

The theme you choose for your space has a lot to do with determining its personality. A bright, fun theme gives an upbeat, high-energy feel; a dark background can give a somber or edgy impression. Choose what fits you today. (You can always change it tomorrow!)

Click the Themes down arrow, and you'll see a series of featured themes at the top of a menu showing categories of theme choices (see Figure 2-9). Click the category you want to see; then click the theme you want to apply to your space. Then watch what happens! The theme is applied instantly to your page, and you can decide whether you want to keep that theme or try another one.

Figure 2-9: Click Themes, and choose first the category and then the color scheme and style you like.

MOVING AND CHANGING MODULES

The different lists and items on your space are called *modules*, and you can create new ones, delete the ones already there, or move them around on your space. Click the

Modules down arrow to see the list of modules on your space. Figure 2-10 shows the list of modules on the sample space. The terms on the right side of the list show what action will be taken when you click that item. (For example, if you clicked Blog in the list shown in the figure, you'd remove the Blog module from the space.) Notice that in addition to the modules created by default (Profile, Photo Album, and Blog, for example), a few custom modules have been added to the sample space (Vegetarian Recipes, Healthy Substitutions, and more).

CHANGING SPACE LAYOUT

Another way you may want to personalize your space involves changing the layout of the entire page. Click the Layout down arrow to see the list of available layout styles (see Figure 2-11), and click the one you want. Experiment with different layouts; to move the modules around on your space, simply click and drag the module to the new position.

When you're finished customizing your space, click Save to save all your changes. Now click Preview My Space to see how your space looks after all your personalizing.

Figure 2-10 (left): Click the Modules down arrow to display and work with the list of items on your space.

Figure 2-11 (right): Click Layout, and choose the grid style you want to use.

MSN SPACES BACKSTORY Q&A

Karen Luk, program manager for MSN Spaces (http://spaces.msn .com/k/), gives her take on the service:

Q: What do you personally like most about MSN Spaces? How do you see it being used two or three years from now?

A: Tough question—there are a lot of things I like about spaces. I love that it's so easy to change things up! With a couple of clicks your space is *totally* different. I love gleams—it's even easier to keep up with the people I care about and a great way to kill time when you're bored or wanting to procrastinate.

I also love the serendipity of discovering little things about people you know by reading their space—the things that you'd never think to ask, the things that someone would never directly offer up in conversation, and the things that when you read them you learn something new and interesting about that person and feel a little more connected to them.

In two to three years, I think it's all about connecting people with other people and information. With a growing amount of information being posted to the Internet, you want to be able to find the things and people you want to find, continue to discover things serendipitously, and see only the information that is relevant to you by filtering out all the noise.

GET HELP IF YOU NEED IT!

MSN Spaces is simple to learn and use, but if Web publishing is new to you, you may appreciate having multiple resources nearby. The MSN Spaces help system is always just a click away, whenever you're working in MSN Spaces. In fact, context-sensitive links appear along the right edge of your screen while you're working on your space. Simply click the question that most closely reflects what you want to know. If you don't see the topic you want to know more about, click in the Search Help box and type a topic you want to see more about; press Enter to search the MSN Spaces help system.

After you find the help you need, be sure to click the Was This Topic Useful? link at the bottom of the help text to provide MSN Spaces with feedback, which is valuable in improving the help experience for all MSN Spaces users.

- **Creating and Editing Your Profile**

- **Determining Who Can See Your Information**

- **Specifying How People Can Contact You**

- **Subscribing to Active Contact Information**

Describing Yourself

CHAPTER 3

Have you ever wanted a way to virtually introduce and describe yourself to others on the Internet? If so, fasten your seatbelt because you're about to learn everything there is to know about the new MSN Profile, a part of MSN Spaces. MSN Profile consists of information you can enter about yourself for others to see and search. You can enter information such as your occupation, interests, photo, and contact details into your profile, and almost all the information you enter has some pretty advanced security so only people you trust will have access to your data.

MSN Profile consists of information you can enter about yourself for others to see and search.

You may be wondering, if MSN Profile consists of personal information used for sharing, then what exactly is the difference between a profile and a space? Well, you can think about it this way: you're described by your profile, but your space is really like your house. It's where you keep all your stuff. It has a door, and you get to decide who can come in and play with your toys. Your space can contain your profile so that people who visit your space can learn more about you, but your space and your profile are different.

A Little **Bit of History**

For years, MSN users have had access to a user profile as part of MSN Member Directory (previously available at http://members .msn.com). MSN Member Directory was a public listing service of profile information for more than 100 million MSN users and a one-stop shop for finding people and learning more about them. MSN Member Directory had fixed categories where users could list themselves—everything from Romance to Hobbies & Crafts—and it provided a way to search for users by the information they entered into their profiles. But MSN Member Directory, as shown in Figure 3-1, is no more; it has been replaced by the new MSN Profile and the search capabilities covered in Chapter 8, "Connecting Spaces and Creating Community." Now you may be asking yourself, if MSN Member Directory had all this cool functionality, why was it replaced? Good question.

Here are some reasons why the new MSN Profile is light years better than its predecessor:

- You can share a greater number of fields with others; before, you were limited to just a handful.

- You can secure information entered into the profile so only people you know and trust will be able to see it. The permissions available range from the most basic ("everyone on the Internet can see my information") to incredibly advanced ("only my mother and people on my MSN Messenger list can see my information").

- The new profile includes the ability to subscribe to other people's contact information as a way to stay up-to-date on changes (we'll discuss Active Contacts soon!).

- The profile information is integrated into MSN Spaces Search (see Chapter 8, "Connecting Spaces and Creating Community"), so you still have access to basic and advanced searches.

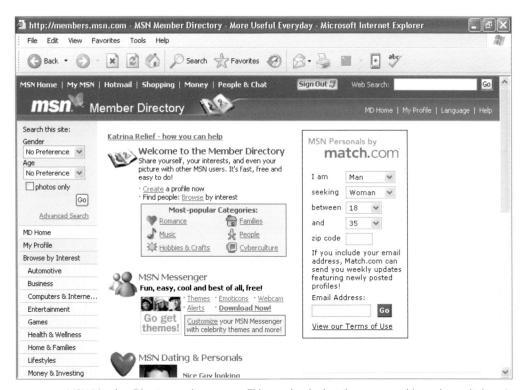

Figure 3-1: MSN Member Directory as it once was. This may be the last time you see this service, as it doesn't exist anymore.

- The user interface is more closely aligned with MSN Spaces. In the past, if you wanted to associate your profile information with your space, you had to bounce around between MSN Spaces and MSN Member Directory. Now, you can do it all from MSN Spaces.

- The new profile is now integrated into the "gleam" and contact card used in MSN Messenger, MSN Spaces, and MSN Hotmail (and also described in Chapter 8, "Connecting Spaces and Creating Community"). This way, your profile isn't an island of information—when you change it, the people you care about will know almost immediately.

> **TIP**
>
> A number of other profile services exist on the Web, although MSN Profile is the only one that can be added to your space. Each profile is a little different from the next, but cumulatively they're used by a large percentage of Internet users. Here are some of the other popular profile services: Friendster (http://www.friendster.com), Orkut (http://www.orkut.com), Yahoo Member Directory (http://members.yahoo.com), Yahoo 360 (http://360.yahoo.com), and LinkedIn (http://www.linkedin.com).

MY INFORMATION IS ALREADY THERE!

As part of the switch from the old profile in MSN Member Directory to the new MSN Profile, if you were an MSN Member Directory user, your information was automatically "moved" from the old to the new service...saving you the trouble of having to enter it again. Of course, your new profile has far more fields for you to use. So, if your information was previously in MSN Member Directory, the only information that will be added to your new profile is information you had there.

This means if you had an old profile containing your location (City, State), your city and state will automatically be added to your new profile. But a field such as Places Lived, which is available only in the new profile, will be blank (since this field wasn't included in your old profile).

Creating and Editing Your Profile

Let's get started with creating your profile, and we'll talk about ways to edit it when the need arises. Creating a profile may take five seconds, or it may take five hours—it all depends on how detailed you want it to be! Since this book is all about MSN Spaces, let's start with first adding the Profile module to your space layout. You can then edit the profile details from there.

To create or edit your profile, follow these steps:

1. From Edit mode of your space, click Customize to start customizing your space.

2. In the Modules drop-down list, click Add next to the word *Profile*. Note that the Profile module may already be shown on your space. If this is the case, you can skip this step.

3. Click Save to save the Profile module to your space.

4. Find the Profile module on the page, and click Edit Profile (or Create Profile if you don't already have one) in the module header (see Figure 3-2). This will bring you to your profile page.

Figure 3-2: Clicking Edit Profile or Create Profile in the header of your Profile module will take you to your profile on MSN Profile.

As soon as you add your profile to your space, it's automatically available on your MSN Spaces home page for visitors to see. If you'd like to move your Profile module around on the page, you'll need to enter Customize mode and place it. (See Chapter 7, "Your Space, Your Way," for more information on layout and customization.)

TIP

On your profile page, you'll see a few different sections of information: Public, General, Social, and Active Contact Information.

PUBLIC AND GENERAL INFORMATION

The information available in the Public section is exactly what it sounds like—information that's always public to the world. This is the only section of the profile that you can't restrict access to; anyone who finds your profile will be able to see the information in this section automatically. For this reason, the information in the Public section is limited and consists only of the name you like to go by.

> NOTE
>
> In some cases, you might see two names in the Public section, a Name field and a Nickname field. This will occur if you either already had a nickname previously or are editing your profile from a service that requires a nickname. (MSN Groups and MSN Chat fall into this category.) If you have a nickname and don't like it, you can change it from this page. You can also remove it completely. The name you enter in the Name field is the one that will be used throughout MSN Spaces. (The Nickname field is pretty much ignored.) And unlike the nickname, your name doesn't have to be unique within the system, so it can be whatever you want it to be.

The Name field is really just a display name for you on MSN. This can be anything you'd like it to be—"ButterflyLover," "Frankie Boombox," your first name, or your full name—but you have to enter *something* (it's mandatory). However, it's up to you how much you'd like to share publicly with people. If you're concerned about privacy, you might want to use just your first name—people who want to know your full name will be able to view it in the Active Contact Information area *if and only if they have access to it.* We'll discuss that in the upcoming "Active Contact Information" section.

The General section consists of optional fields, and you can limit who can see this information (see Figure 3-3).

The following are the fields in the General Information section:

Photo This is a photo that represents you on your space as well as throughout other experiences on MSN. Choose this one wisely, as it appears in a bunch of places. To upload a profile photo, click Browse, and find an appropriate photo on

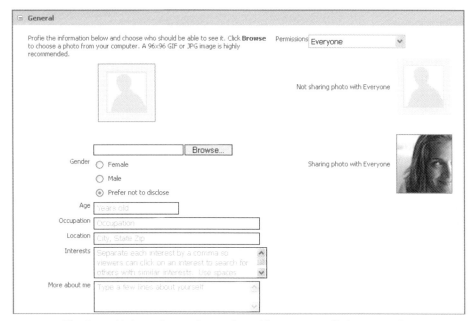

Figure 3-3: The General Information section can be public, or you can limit access to it.

your hard drive. It's recommended that you use a 96×96 photograph (96 pixels wide and 96 pixels high) in GIF or JPG format. Either format works and won't likely have a noticeable difference visually, but you might want to use the JPG format to ensure a lower file size (and quicker downloads!). To learn more about working with photos, please refer to Chapter 5, "Sharing Your Photos."

Gender   Your gender. The choices are Male, Female, or Prefer Not To Disclose.

Age   How old you are. The permitted age range is from 18 to 255. (If you live to be 255 years old, you better blog about it!).

Occupation   What you do for a living, for example, "Architect" or "Teacher."

Location   Where you live. "City, State, Zip" is the suggested format for your location.

Interests   Your interests will be automatically linked from your profile to other people with similar interests when your profile is being viewed. Interests will also be used to determine the most popular interests on the Interests page. (See

Chapter 8, "Connecting Spaces and Creating Community," for more information about the Interests page.)

More About Me   This field is the one most people tend to enjoy because it's open ended; you can enter whatever you want other people to know about you in this textbox.

Remember, you can fill in all these fields, you can fill in only the ones most important to you, or you can leave them all alone.

BEING SOCIAL!

One of the sections in your profile, the Social section, is all about describing yourself for the purpose of meeting new people or giving people you already know something to talk about! You can think of it as a section full of conversation starters. Here are the fields in the Social section:

- Marital Status
- Interested In (friends, activity partners, business networking, dating)
- Pets (Yes, "No, but I would love to," or "No, and I don't want them")
- Hometown
- Places Lived
- Humor (friendly, goofy, obscure, and so on)
- Fashion (unique, classy, trendy, and so on)
- Music (classical, hip-hop, living in the 80s, and so on)
- Favorite Quote

Just like the General section, all this information is optional. So, fill in only the fields you're comfortable sharing with other people.

ACTIVE CONTACT INFORMATION

Active Contacts is a new service provided by MSN that automatically keeps your contact information up-to-date in other people's address books! It's a pretty powerful concept and incredibly useful for friends and family of college kids and constant nomads. The data you enter into the Active Contact Information section of your profile is the information that will be used to keep your friends' and family's address books current. The fields span both personal and work information (see Figure 3-4). Just like the General and Social sections, the information you enter into your Active Contact Information section can be public or private—you don't have to make this information available to the whole world. We'll talk more about permissions in a minute when we get to the "Specifying Who Can See Your Information" section.

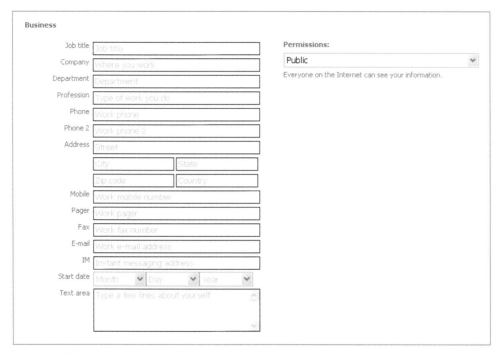

Figure 3-4: The Active Contact Information section consists of personal and business contact information. The business section shown here contains similar fields as personal but geared more toward professional use.

WHAT IS MY PHOTO USED FOR?

Your photo will be used in a number of places if your general profile is shared publicly. It will be shown in MSN Spaces Search results when your space or profile is returned as a match. (See Chapter 8, "Connecting Spaces and Creating Community," for more information about MSN Spaces Search.) It will also be used in the Friends module if you're a mutual friend of someone. And you have the option of leaving it behind when you comment on blog entries or photos. Additionally, if you add the Profile module to your space, then your photo will also appear on the home page of your space.

But it actually isn't just your profile photo you're leaving behind; it's also a way for people to learn more about you. Each time your profile photo appears, people have the option of viewing your contact card, inviting you to MSN Messenger, viewing your profile or your space, and more! All of this functionality is possible only if the viewer has the rights to perform it.

Jay Fluegel, a lead program manager for MSN Spaces, describes it this way: "MSN is about you and your relationships. There are people at Microsoft who spend countless hours making MSN a fun place for you to stay connected with the people you care about most. With that in mind, we made sure that any time you come across a person in MSN Messenger or one of our Web sites like MSN Spaces or Hotmail, you see that person's picture, can view his or her contact card, or start an activity with him or her." You can visit Jay on his space; just browse on over to http://spaces.msn.com/jay.

SPECIFYING WHO CAN SEE YOUR INFORMATION

Permission settings are an integral part of MSN Profile in that they give you complete control over who can see your personal information. Without permissions, all your profile data would be shared with anyone with an Internet connection. While this might be OK for some people, many people aren't comfortable with complete strangers knowing that they like cheesy 1980s music and named their cats Madonna and Duran Duran. So, for this reason, you're able to specify who can see your stuff.

The Permissions drop-down list to the right of the profile sections has a couple options (see Figure 3-5) that map almost exactly to the permissions options for your space.

Figure 3-5: The Permissions drop-down list includes many standard options and the option of selecting Custom to go à la carte.

Each setting is slightly different from the one before it:

Same As Space   This option will let you maintain one list of people you trust—the people you have already said can see your space. This one isn't available in MSN Spaces permissions.

Messenger   This option will limit access to your information to just the people on your MSN Messenger Allow List. Whenever you add someone to your MSN Messenger contact list, you automatically grant them access to your information.

Messenger & Friends   This option combines your trusted private network (MSN Messenger) with your trusted public network (your friends). Whenever you add someone to either list, you automatically grant them access to your information.

Messenger, Friends, & Mutual Friends of Friends   This option really means "the mutual friends of your mutual friends" and your friends. Kind of like the Six Degrees of Separation—but in this case it's the two degrees of you!

Public   Public to the world!

You can also select Custom, which gives you à la carte access to your permission settings.

Custom permissions give you complete control over all the previous options with the additional capability of a "people picker" that enables you to select individual contacts (see Figure 3-6). This option, just like the drop-down list just discussed, is the same as in MSN Spaces permissions. With custom permissions, you can mix and match the options to create your own permissions soup. For example, you can do the following: "My mother and brother have access to my personal contact information and my MSN Messenger Allow list. Joe has access to my social information, and everyone has access to my business contact information." This might sound a little out of control, but when it comes to your personal data, you should have as many options as possible for determining who can see it.

Figure 3-6: Total control over who can see your stuff—choose from a menu of options.

HOW TO VIEW PEOPLE'S PROFILES

Profiles are shared in a bunch of places throughout MSN. If you're looking to learn a little bit more about someone, you can find their profile pretty easily depending on where you are. Here are a few places you can find someone's profile:

MSN Spaces Search   Each time you search for someone from http://spaces.msn .com, you're presented with a list of profile photos. Each photo has a list of actions associated with it—just hover your mouse pointer over the photo, and click the "actions" arrow below the photo (note: you can also right-click). One of the actions in the list is View Profile, which will open this user's profile on MSN Profile.

MSN Spaces (of course!)   If someone has a profile, they may have added it to their space. If so, you should see it on their home page. If they have a profile but haven't added it to their space, you'll still see a link to the profile in the top header on their space (next to Blog, Photos, and so on). You can also open someone's profile from the Friends module or when reading a comment that contains someone's profile photo. Just like with MSN Spaces Search, hover your mouse pointer over their photo, and click the "actions" arrow below the photo. Clicking View Profile from here will open this user's profile.

MSN Messenger   If you right-click any contact in your contact list, you can select View Profile, which opens their profile page. You can also see someone's profile if you're viewing their friends list (right-click, and select View Friends)— all you have to do is hover your mouse pointer over their photo, and click the "actions" arrow below the photo. Clicking View Photo from here will open this user's profile.

COMMUNICATION PREFERENCES: STOP BUGGING ME!

One of the potential downsides to being discoverable via MSN Spaces Search or other people's friends lists is that you could be inundated with requests to be a mutual friend, an active contact, or an MSN Messenger contact. Of course, if you're interested in meeting new people or being discovered by old friends, this might be exactly what you want. But if you're Britney Spears or Bill Gates, this is a problem you'd probably rather not have. Thankfully, you have another way to specify who can contact you: communication preferences. With communication preferences, you have complete control over how you'd like to be notified, if at all.

You can get to communication preferences in a few ways:

- Link from Settings (in Edit mode of your space) or from your profile page.

- Link from the bottom of every e-mail you receive from MSN Spaces.

- Type **http://spaces.msn.com/commpref.aspx** into your Web browser's address bar.

These are the preferences you can set on this page:

- Who can invite you to be an MSN Messenger contact

- Who can invite you to be a mutual friend

- Who can request access to your space

- Who can request to be an active contact

This page is your friend—if you ever find yourself being annoyed by the number of requests you're getting, you can tweak the settings to be a little stricter. The options available to you depend on the setting you're changing, but they map almost exactly to the permissions options described in the "Specifying Who Can See Your Information" section.

Active Contacts: Subscribing to Updates

How many times have you called the wrong number or sent a letter to the wrong address just because your friend was too lazy to let you know they moved? With the Active Contacts feature, this may *never* have to happen again. You now have the ability to exchange contact information with your friends and family automatically— so every time your contact information changes, your friends see the changes in their address book, and vice versa! Pretty cool.

Subscribing to someone's active contact information is easy. All you have to do is select Make This An Active Contact from the Actions menu associated with a user's photo in MSN Spaces Search, the Friends module, or the Profile module shown on their space. (To see the Actions menu, just hover your mouse pointer over a user's photo wherever you see it, and click the "actions" arrow below the photo. A Web page will open and take you to a screen similar to the one shown in Figure 3-7.)

NOTE If you don't already have access to someone's active contact information (either personal or business), a request will be sent asking them to grant you access. This request may never actually reach them depending on how they have configured their communication preferences. For example, if they have specified that only MSN Messenger contacts can request to be an active contact, and you aren't an MSN Messenger contact of this user, your request will be ignored. Either way, a contact will be created in your address book for this user.

After you have opted to make someone an active contact, the information you have access to (personal and/or business contact information) will automatically appear in your address book. If you don't have access to any of the user's contact information, the contact record for this user will be mostly blank (except for his or her name). But as soon as they give you access to their contact information, their contact record in your address book will magically fill in and stay up-to-date!

TIP You can view your address book in MSN Messenger or MSN Hotmail (http://www.hotmail.com).

The following contact will be added to your address book and set to receive automatic updates when he or she updates his or her contact information:

Display in your address book as:

Mikey

First name   Last name

Mike   **Torres**

You choose the display name of the contact in your address book so you can easily find it when you need it. Your contact may update the first and last name fields at any time.

Click **Next** to save the changes above.

[Next]   [Cancel]

Figure 3-7: Click a profile photo, and select the action to make the user an active contact.

REPORTING PROBLEMS

Every once in a while you might experience a hiccup with MSN Spaces. This could be anything from "service not available" to "page not found" errors. You may also have problems with abusive users—people who are leaving threatening comments on your space or people promoting or sharing something illegal on their space. In all cases, Microsoft has resources available to you should you want to engage the Support team to help resolve your problems. You can contact Microsoft Support by clicking the Feedback or Report Abuse links at the bottom of any space. In both cases you'll be presented with a Web form to complete.

If you're just looking for help from other MSN Spaces users, your best bet is to use the MSN Spaces Search tool available at http://spaces.msn.com. Make sure to optimize your search query to make sure you find what you want. For example, if you're looking for information about playing video on your space, you should search for *play video on space* or *Windows Media PowerToy*. (PowerToys are covered in Appendix B, "Advanced MSN Spaces—Undocumented!")

Your last resort is to check out the MSN Spaces team space, available at http://spaces .msn.com/members/thespacecraft. From there you can find the people who work on MSN Spaces. Most of them blog frequently (and are online all day), so you can always post a comment to see whether they can help. Or, if other readers on these spaces have encountered some of the same problems, they might be able to help as well.

Adding and Editing Blog Entries

CHAPTER 4

Your blog entries are the heart of your space...they're where you tell your stories, share your interests, welcome your readers, ask questions, and report on current events. Your blog entries are all about *voice*—your voice, however you want it to sound on your space.

Your blog entries are all about voice— your voice.

If you've spent time surfing through even a portion of the millions of spaces already published, you'll see a huge range of styles, approaches, topics, and uses. Some people post photos as the main part of their space and add blog entries only occasionally. Others blog every day (or close to it), sharing news about what's happening in their lives, their views on current events, recent musings, or odd or happy occurrences. Whatever interests you, you're sure to find a blog about it: you'll find blogs about families, dating, divorce recovery, single parenting, high-school and college experiences, traveling, farming, day dreaming, and much more.

But no matter what *you* want to write about, one important two-part question will help define your space: (1) what caught your attention today, (2) and what do you want to say about it?

TIP

Get in the habit of noticing what you're thinking about throughout the day. It could be great material for your blog. Notice your random thoughts when you're at a stoplight, when you're exercising, or when you're listening to music. Maybe even carry a small notebook to jot down your ideas and capture them for later. Then consider sharing those inner observations with the readers of your space.

Getting Started Blogging

As you learned in Chapter 1, "Introducing MSN Spaces," blogging is a personal publishing phenomenon that has spread throughout the world and into the mainstream in the last few years. Blogging enables you to publish your thoughts—quickly and easily—and make them available on the Web to anyone who wants to view them. (You can control this, too, by setting the permissions level on your space to allow the public or only selected people to view what you post. See Chapter 2, "Getting a Space of Your Own," for more information.)

> You'll see the term *blog* used in several ways. Some folks refer to each entry on their space as *a blog*, but the blog itself is actually the entire module (the list in which all the entries appear); each entry is called, logically enough, a *blog entry*. We also distinguish *blog* from *space* in that your space is your entire MSN Spaces site, with lists, a photo album, a profile, a blog, and more.

NOTE

To begin working on your first blog entry, follow these steps:

1. Sign in to your space. Your space appears in Edit mode.

2. Find the Blog list, and click Add Entry. The Edit Blog Entry window appears (see Figure 4-1 on the following page).

The date is entered automatically for you, but you'll be adding the title, selecting the category, and entering the text for the blog entry in the next sections.

Titling Your Blog Entry

Creating a fun, lively, or attention-getting title is half the trick to getting your space noticed. And if you update regularly and create interesting titles that hook the reader's curiosity, you increase your chances of developing a devoted and consistent readership for your space. Consider the difference between these two titles:

- "What I did today"

- "Swerving to avoid an elephant"

Which blog entry are you more likely to read? The "What I did today" title may be accurate and fit the content of what you actually want to write about; but if you were driving a golf cart at the zoo and had to swerve to miss the baby elephant,

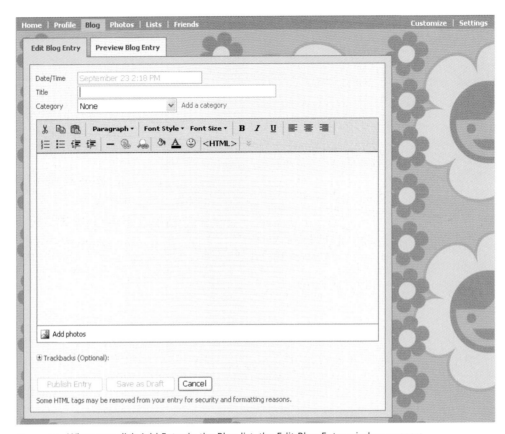

Figure 4-1: When you click Add Entry in the Blog list, the Edit Blog Entry window appears.

now *that's* something to write about! The second title also brings up a strong image in the reader's mind, which is a powerful way to connect with your space visitors. Show them in words what you want them to see, and they're likely to remember—and enjoy—what you describe. Leave it too vague or uninteresting (each of us had stuff we did today that we could put in that first blog entry), and readers may not think your space is worth the trouble.

To add the title, click in the Title box, and type the text you want to appear as the title. It's that simple.

DOWNPLAYING THE DATE

Not everybody is cut out to add new blog entries every day. If you're like most people, you'll have time to update the blog on your space two to three times a week. But some folks don't add anything for weeks at a time. If you're an as-needed blogger (meaning that you update your site only once in a while, when you have something new to say), you may be interested in listing the entries on your space not by date but by topic. You can change the way your blog entries are organized by clicking Edit Your Space, choosing Settings, clicking the Blog Settings tab, and changing the setting in the blog entry date display area. By default, the date is displayed at the top of the entry; if you want to downplay *when* you post (making *what* you post the most important part), click Show Date In Footer. After you make the change, scroll down to the bottom of the page, and click Save to preserve your settings.

Choosing a Category

When you first set up your space, MSN Spaces gives you a list of standard categories you can use to identify the basic content of your blog entry. Why are categories important? Well, readers who are interested in a certain topic can search your blog entries by the category you specify. MSN Spaces offers you a dozen categories right off the bat—with topics ranging from Books to Travel—but if you don't see one you want, you can create your own. To choose the category you want to assign to your blog entry, click the Category down arrow, and select the category from the list.

If you don't see a category that fits what you want to write about, click Add A Category, and type a name for a category you want. Click OK to save and apply the new category to your current entry.

> You can have up to 25 categories on your space, and you can delete any of the ones you don't use. When you delete a category, the blog entry assigned to that category doesn't disappear—only the category itself is removed (meaning your site visitors will no longer be able to use that category to sort your entries).

TIP

Entering Text

Now you're ready for the fun part! What's on your mind today? And what do you want to say about it? The blog entry area is wide open, ready for you to pour your inspiration into. Just click in the box, and start typing. Press Enter at the end of your paragraph, and press Enter again to add a blank line between paragraphs if that's your style. Figure 4-2 shows a sample blog entry.

Adding Formatting Touches

The editing tools at the top of the blog entry area provide what you need to apply special formats to your blog text. You can change the size, color, and style of the text; cut and paste text; change the alignment; create numbered and bulleted lists; add smileys; and more. Figure 4-3 shows the various tools available.

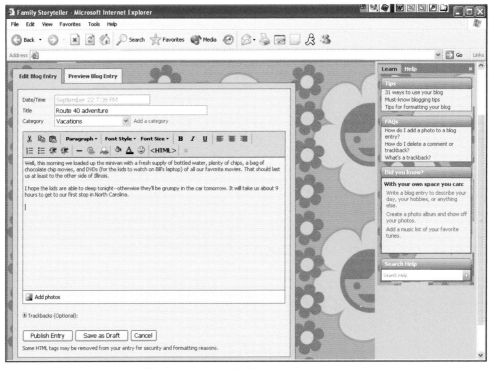

Figure 4-2: Type your text, pressing Enter at the end of paragraphs.

WHOSE VOICE IS THIS, ANYWAY?

One of the fun freedoms—and challenging controversies—of life on the Web is that even though we can't see each other in real time, we can connect through stories, information, and electronic images and words. This means we may be just the way we present ourselves to be—or we may not be that way at all. As you create your space, you may want to share what's going on with you—what you care about, what you're interested in, or what you did today. You may want your writing voice to sound just the way your actual voice sounds, in which case you should write with the same phrases and basic speaking style you use when you're talking one-on-one with a friend.

But in other cases, you might want to adopt a slightly different tone, perhaps giving your edgier, funnier side a chance to show up on your space. One teacher who writes regularly on her space says she's cynical and sarcastic on her blog because she can't be that way in the classroom. Her writing is sharp, is edgy, and still rings true. But the voice she's using isn't the everyday Jane she appears to be in the classroom. She's a teacher with attitude!

When you're thinking through the voice for your blog, be creative! Have fun! Be yourself—or somebody else. Sooner or later, you'll discover the voice that feels most comfortable for you, and it will most likely be the one everybody likes to read.

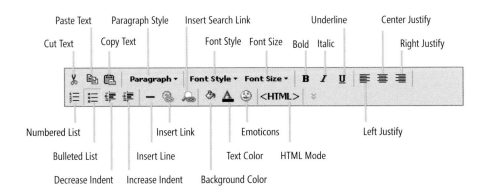

Figure 4-3: Use the formatting tools in the Edit Blog Entry window to apply special formats to your blog text.

You can use these tools to change the format of your text in two ways:

- Highlight the text you want to change, and click the formatting tool you want to use. (For example, highlight a sentence, and click the Bulleted List tool to apply the bullet format to the text you selected.)

- Click at the point in the entry where you want to add formatting, select a tool, and then enter the text. (For example, to add a bullet point, place your cursor where you want to insert a bullet, click the Bulleted List tool, and then type the sentence, as shown in Figure 4-4.)

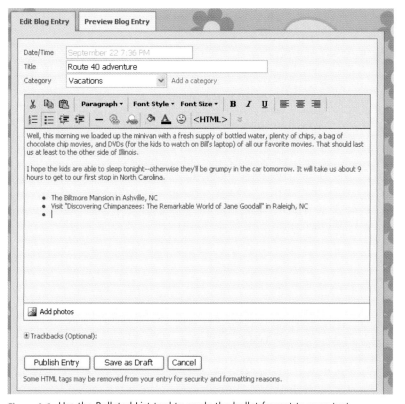

Figure 4-4: Use the Bulleted List tool to apply the bullet format to your text.

Experiment with the formatting tools to get familiar with the way they work on your blog text. The Text Color tool can help you emphasize words; the Emoticon tool lets others know when you're kidding (☺); and the Font Style and Font Size tools give you flexibility in the way your text looks overall. Figure 4-5 shows the effect of the Paragraph Style tool when it's used to add a heading to the blog entry.

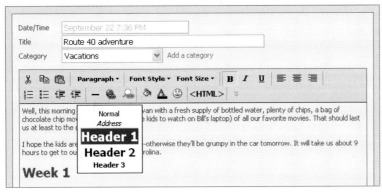

Figure 4-5: Use the Paragraph Style tool to apply a preset format—in a particular font style and size—to your blog text.

Adding Links

Because the Web *is* the Web, you can find related content for virtually anything you write about online. If you're writing about a baseball game you went to the other night, you can link to the Web site of the team; if you're writing about having the flu (sorry to hear that!), you can link to a medical site that lists flu symptoms; if you're talking about some cool new shoes you just bought (or are thinking about buying), you can link to the manufacturer's marketing spin on those shoes; and if you're writing about politics or news—well, you know you can find those topics anywhere on the Web.

Adding links to your blog entries increases your connectivity with other sites and increases the number of people who may stumble upon your blog. Think of adding links as building sidewalks from one place to another—when you link to another site, you provide a path to your blog that didn't exist before. Not everyone will use that path; many people might not know it's there, but certain online tools (Technorati.com, for one) report on the number of links to particular sites and can help get your space noticed.

TIP

If you want to provide your visitors with more information about a certain topic but don't want to spend hours scouring the Web for just the right site, you can use the Insert Search Link tool to do the searching for you. Just highlight the text you want to search for, and click the Insert Search Link tool in the Formatting toolbar. MSN Spaces adds a link to the MSN Search page with the results already compiled and linked to the word you selected. Amazing! It's fast and easy, and you've just given your visitors another reason to love your space.

Adding a link to your blog entry is simple. Here's how to do it:

① Select the text you want to use as the clickable part of the link (where you want your blog readers to click in order to move to the other site).

② Click the Insert Link tool in the Formatting toolbar above the blog entry area.

③ Type the site's URL in the Insert Hyperlink box that appears, as shown in Figure 4-6.

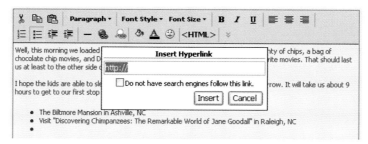

Figure 4-6: Type or copy the URL from the other site into the Insert Hyperlink box.

You may want to have two browser windows open so you can simply copy and paste the URL from the other site into your MSN Spaces blog entry.

4 Click Insert. The link is added to your blog entry, highlighted in a different color to show readers that it's a link.

If you're interested in keeping your space quiet, click the Do Not Have Search Engines Follow This Link checkbox. This keeps Internet search engines from picking up on your space through the other sites to which you may be linking. Of course, if you *do* want the traffic (linking to other sites is a great way to get your space noticed!), leave the checkbox unchecked.

TIP

How many links is too many? We have no rule for this, but remember that you want people coming to your space because they want to see what *you've* posted, and links take people to another site. So link away, but remember to provide good content of your own so people keep returning to your space.

TIP

Adding Images

We talk about photos in detail in Chapter 5, "Sharing Your Photos," so we'll give you only the quick version of the steps here so you can see how the whole process fits together. The photos you add to your blog entries provide an extra dimension to the words you're writing because they can actually take the reader into the experience in a more realistic way. When you talk about how cold the lake water was when you fell out of the fishing boat, readers will be able to identify—but they will smile, or laugh, or think "Brrr!" if they're able to see a photo of you falling backward into the water. (How much would you pay to keep *that* photo off the Internet?!) You've heard the cliché "A picture is worth a thousand words," and perhaps it's a cliché because it's true. Adding photos offers impact that words don't necessarily have alone.

To add a photo to your blog entry, follow these steps:

1. Click Add Photos at the bottom of the blog entry area.

2. When the Add Photos window appears, navigate in the left panel to the folder containing the images you want to add.

3. Select the photos by clicking the checkboxes in the upper-left corner of each image.

   You can also do some editing here if you like, but see Chapter 5, "Sharing Your Photos," for those details.

4. Click Upload Now to add the photos to your space (see Figure 4-7).

Figure 4-7: Upload photos to your blog entry by selecting them in the Add Photos window and clicking Upload Now.

POWER USER TIP: ADDING INLINE PHOTOS

If you're comfortable working with Hypertext Markup Language (HTML), you can add your photos within the body of your blog entry. Start your entry as usual, adding the title and category. Then click the HTML Mode button to display the HTML code for the blog entry. Position the cursor where you want the image to appear in your blog entry, and then enter this command:

<img src="http://*URL-to-the-server/image.jpg*" border=0>

In the preceding command line, the "img" part refers to "image," and the "src" part refers to "source." The next part is the address of the server where the image is stored. Substitute the URL where your image is stored and the filename of your photo for the italic phrases in the command line. If you want to change the height and width of the image, you specify the height and width (in pixels) of the image size you want (something like "height=250" and "width=300"). For example, the syntax of an inline image might look like this:

<img src="http://www.mysite.picnic.jpg" border=0 height=250 width=300>

You may have to experiment with the size and placement of the image, but it's a fun technique, and—the best part—it gives you more control over the photos on your space!

The filenames of the photos appear beneath the Add Photos link in the blog entry area. If you find that you've added a photo or two you really don't want to keep, you can easily delete the photos you've added by clicking the *X* in the Delete Photo column to the right of the image filename (see Figure 4-8).

In the finished blog entry, the added photos will appear at the end of the entry, and readers will be able to enlarge a photo by clicking the one they want to see. Additionally, the photos will appear in a photo album called My Blog Photos, so visitors will also be able to view the images you add to your blog entries in a slide show.

Add photos	
Photos added	Delete photo
sunflower field	X
on the road	X
bison	X

Figure 4-8: Remove an unwanted photo by clicking the *X* to the right of the image filename.

TIP One of the fun ways to get visitors engaged with what you post is to read and respond to the photo comments feature available with each photo on your blog. Try using the photo comments feature, and see what happens!

Previewing and Publishing the Entry

You're almost finished! Once you have all the text in place and formatted the way you want, and you've added any photos you want to include, you can see the way your blog entry will look by clicking the Preview Blog Entry tab at the top of the blog entry area. You'll see how the entry will appear to others when they visit your site (see Figure 4-9).

If you're happy with what you see, click Publish Entry to finalize your work; if not, click Save As Draft if you want to return to the blog entry and work on it more.

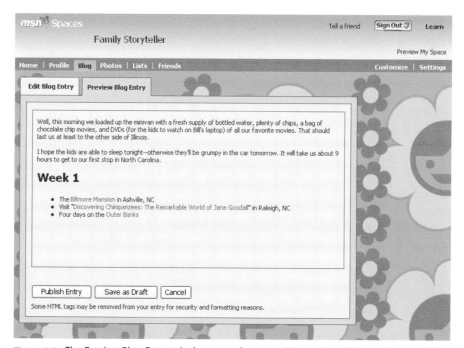

Figure 4-9: The Preview Blog Entry tab shows you how your blog entry will look after you click Publish Entry.

Editing Entries

After you click Publish Entry, the blog entry is saved, and the title of the entry is listed in Edit mode (see Figure 4-10). If you want to change the blog entry (now or later), simply click the entry title (in this case, Route 40 Adventure), and the entry will open in the Edit Blog Entry window so you can make the changes you want to make.

If you decide you really don't want to keep the entry you've created, you can delete it by clicking the X in the Delete column.

Figure 4-10: You'll see the finished blog entry listed under Recent Entries in the Blog list in Edit mode.

> If you change a blog entry after posting it, it's best to simply add to the information you've already posted. We typically use a different font and add "Update:" or "New development:" before the new text so readers will know we're enhancing—not recanting—an earlier blog entry. (It's always fine to make punctuation corrections and such, though!)
>
> TIP

Exploring the How-tos of Mobile Blogging

In Chapter 2, "Getting a Space of Your Own," you learned how to set up your space for mobile blogging. Mobile blogging is posting to your space by using a cell phone, smartphone, or personal digital assistant (PDA) with Internet capability. If your phone has the capacity to send multimedia messages (text and images), you may be able to "phone in" your blog entries.

Here's the process in a nutshell:

1. Make sure your space's settings support mobile blogging. (See Chapter 2 for specific details on how to do this.)

2. Make a special note of the e-mail address MSN Spaces gives you at the bottom of the E-mail Publishing page; this is the e-mail address to which you'll send your blog entry.

   In fact, to make mobile blogging easier, you may want to create a contact for this number in your phone so it's ready when you need it.

3. On your phone, select the necessary option to create an e-mail message.

   The options you select for this varies from phone to phone.

4. Type your text, add a photo if you want, and press Send.

5. Choose the contact you created for the MSN Spaces e-mail address that will post to your blog, and click OK to send the message.

The message is sent to your blog, and depending on whether you selected Save Entries As Drafts or Publish Immediately on the E-mail Publishing tab, either the blog entry will be saved for you to edit and publish when you return to your space or it will be posted immediately online.

MSN SPACES BACKSTORY: SEE MSN SPACES GROW!

Moz Hussain, a product manager for MSN Spaces (http://spaces. msn.com/members/mozatwork/), talks about the growth of MSN Spaces:

Q: Has the popularity of MSN Spaces surpassed your original expectations?

A: The first forecast for MSN Spaces (in December 2004) predicted that realizing six million spaces by June 2005 would be an aggressive goal. We reached that number by early April, blowing away everyone's expectations. At one point, the operations team was adding a terabyte (one trillion bytes!) of new storage every nine days as photo upload volume reached ten million photos per day! The growth surprised the team but renewed our belief in the product and led to even higher goals.

Q: MSN Spaces is great, and it's also free to users (which is great for us!). But how will MSN Spaces be able to continue if it's a free service?

A: Early on, the Spaces team realized that you could make money by giving people a great experience. The two aren't mutually exclusive. For example, the Volvo "What's Your Story?" deal is a fantastic example of how you can combine an advertiser proposition and create something compelling for users. The "What's Your Story?" hub has had more than 4 million visitors and more than 75 percent satisfaction rate, one of the highest in MSN. It showcases the best of MSN Spaces and connects and inspires users while allowing our advertising partner to connect with users in a new and exciting way.

Q: It seems like MSN Spaces has caught on all over the world. What are you doing to help MSN Spaces grow in other countries?

A: Our marketing team conducted detailed research in the UK, China, Japan, and Brazil to study the potential of MSN Spaces in each market. The results of that study highlighted critical cultural differences that the team now takes into account in developing the product. For example, Japanese users were OK with strangers reading their blog but didn't want their friends, family, or co-workers being notified when they updated their spaces. This is completely different from the rest of the world and highlights the challenge of developing global products.

Thanks, Moz, for sharing your insider's view with us!

- **Uploading Photos and Creating Photo Albums**
- **Viewing Your Photos in Three Ways**
- **Editing Your Photos**
- **Saving Photo Comments**

Sharing Your Photos

CHAPTER 5

Telling your story is a great way to connect with friends and family, but *showing* your story really takes people there. You might write about the scary experience of crossing a rope bridge in Costa Rica last summer, but your viewers will feel their world spin right alongside yours if you can show them in your photos what the view was from that height! And that's what photos are all about: sharing your experience in a powerful way.

Telling your story is a great way to connect with friends and family, but showing your story really takes people there.

MSN Spaces makes posting and sharing your photos incredibly easy—and gives you a lot of flexibility in the way you display them. Unlike other blogging programs, MSN Spaces gives you both the space and the easy-to-use upload utility that helps you organize, store, name, and even edit the photos you post online. What's more, you can invite others into your story by letting them add comments to your favorite photos and link to their own spaces where they can show you *their* photos.

How Will You Use Photos on Your Space?

Visit almost any space on MSN Spaces and you're sure to find photos of all kinds—big photos, small photos, photos as part of blog entries, photos in photo albums. Some people resize their photo album to take up the lion's share of space on their screen; others keep the photo album small and simple—but always updated, tucked away in a corner of their space.

Whether you created your space to showcase your favorite photos, to write about the happenings in your life, to share information with family scattered all over the globe, or to develop a fun social network about a particular interest or hobby you have, working with photos is sure to be an important and creative part of the way you express yourself.

GREAT NEW PHOTO OPS IN MSN SPACES

MSN Spaces includes some great new photo features that give you additional choices for the way you view, organize, use, and interact with photos on your space:

Montage view displays a collection of your photos in reduced, thumbnail size.

Social networking enables you to connect to others through photos of your friends (and *their* friends!).

Commenting on photos means your friends and family can add fun notes, captions, and questions to the photos on your space.

Photo descriptions enable you to add a lengthy caption to describe the experience or add your own thoughts

Flipping through the Photo Album

It all begins with the little Photo Album area in the top-right corner of your space. When you first create your space, the Photo Album area is empty—it's nothing more than a placeholder where you'll eventually show the world what you want it to see.

After you add a few photos—either by posting them with your blog entries or by creating a photo album, you'll use the navigation buttons beneath the displayed image to flip through the photos. As you create additional photo albums, you'll see them appear beneath the image that is displayed in Slideshow view (see Figure 5-1).

The photos in the selected album display as a slide show montage, a collection of photos you've added to that particular album. You can enlarge a specific photo by positioning the mouse pointer over it; the photo magnifies while you're pointing at it. If you want to display your photos in Slideshow view, click the down-arrow to the right of Montage in the Photo Album title bar and click Slideshow. Each photo appears for approximately five seconds, and then (if the album has more than one photo) the next photo displays. The navigation buttons enable you to move to the photos you most want to see: Pause stops cycling the display and freezes the image on the current photo, Stop ends the slide show altogether, Previous shows the photo immediately preceding the current one, and Next displays the photo next in line to be displayed. Nothing is too surprising here. These navigation options appear automatically; you don't need to do anything except upload the photos you want everyone to see.

Click to change to Slideshow view

Point to photo to enlarge it

Figure 5-1: The Photo Album displays your photos in Montage view, showing thumbnails of all the images you've added.

CREATING AN ONLINE PHOTO ALBUM

Because MSN Spaces makes it so easy to upload, edit, store, and share photos, one of the first tasks most of us do is create a photo album of our favorite images. Some people create photo blogs that are more image than text and upload photos from all over—posting the latest images from cell phones, personal digital assistants (PDAs), webcams, and scanners and showing the world what's happening in their lives.

What makes a good photo album? The answer is, just about anything—any topic, person, place, or event you want to share. You might create a photo album to show the ten finest photos from your best friend's wedding shower. Or you might create a photo album about the weekend you took your son to camp. Or you might simply have one photo album for each of your best friends—or your pets. Whatever the topic of the album, the idea is to group photos in such a way that the folks viewing them will understand how they're connected. You might even simply do a "day-in-the-life" photo album that shows images you captured throughout a single day.

When you're ready to create a photo album for your space, follow these steps:

① Click Edit Your Space in the upper-right corner of your space.

② Click the Create link that appears beneath the Photo Album heading.

③ In the Create Photo Album window, enter a name for the photo album you're creating.

④ Now click Add Photos at the top of New Album window (see Figure 5-2). The Add Photos window appears so that you can choose the photos you want to include in your new album.

⑤ Using the folder list in the left panel of the Add Photos window (see Figure 5-3), navigate to the folder containing the photos you want to add.

⑥ Click the checkbox in the upper-left corner of a photo to select it. Click any additional photos you want to include in the photo album.

⑦ Click Upload Now to add the selected photo(s) to your blog.

A status window shows you what's happening as the photos are copied to your space. When the window closes, you're returned to the New Album window.

⑧ Click Save and Close to save your album and view it on your space.

To get the full effect of your new album, click Preview My Space to cycle through the images you've added.

TIP
MSN Spaces gives you a generous amount of space, but it's always a good idea to compress your photos before uploading them. MSN Spaces actually does some compressing for you by converting and reducing the size of images as soon as you upload them, but compressing photo files is a good practice to adopt for those times when you're e-mailing or uploading images to other sites. Photos can make for huge files and tie up transmission times—especially if some of your friends have dial-up connections.

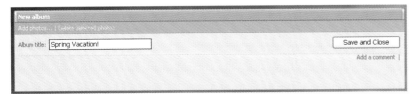

Figure 5-2: In the New Album window, enter a title for the album, and click Add Photos to select the images you want to show.

Figure 5-3: The Add Photos window enables you to select, edit, and upload new photos for your album.

EDITING, REORGANIZING, AND DELETING ALBUMS

After you create a photo album, you may find that you want to edit the photo name, change the order of photos, or remove some images you included. You'll always have fine-tuning to do! Later in this chapter you'll learn how to work with individual photos, and here we'll focus on working with the albums you create.

THIS IS GREAT! HOW DO I MAKE THE PHOTO ALBUM BIGGER?

As you're browsing other people's spaces, you may notice that some people love their photo albums so much they make them big enough to fill practically the whole space. If you want to make your photo album larger, you can change the layout of your space to give the photo album more room. We'll show you how to do this in Chapter 7, "Your Space, Your Way."

Part of the flexibility of MSN Spaces is that it gives you more than one way to do what you want to do. When you want to make changes to a photo album, you can either work with the photo album on the main page or click the Photos tab (across the top of the space, just beneath the space title).

The easiest way to edit your photo album is to click Edit Your Space, select the album you want to change, and click Edit. The Edit Album window opens so that you can rename the album or individual photos, add or remove photos, or rearrange the photos in the album.

To rename your photo album, click in the Album Title box and type the new name for the album. Click Save and Close to finalize your changes and return to Edit mode.

If you want to change the order of the photo albums in the Photo Album list, simply click the album you want to move, and drag it up or down in the album list. After you release the mouse button, the photo album will move to the new location.

Finally, if you want to delete an album, click the album you want to remove in the Photo Album list, and click Delete. (If you don't see Delete as an option, make sure you have clicked Edit Your Space.) MSN Spaces displays a confirmation message asking whether you want to continue with the deletion. If you do, click Yes; otherwise, click No.

A Space with Three Views: Slideshow, Montage, and Full View

Now that you know how to create a photo album for your space, you have probably uploaded some photos that make you smile. MSN Spaces has several ways to enjoy your photos. You can view them in the photo album as just described, or you can display them in one of three views: Slideshow, Montage, or Full. You can switch between views by clicking the view's down arrow in the upper-right corner of the photo album. Clicking the view displays a short menu, and you can choose the view in which you want your photos to be displayed (see Figure 5-4). The down arrow on the left side of the photo album enables you to choose the photo album you want to display.

As you see in Figure 5-4, Slideshow view displays your images one at a time and rotates through the images, displaying each one in the Photo Album area. When you display the photos in Full view, the photo album opens in the Photo tab, displaying a larger image, the filename or caption underneath, and a navigation bar that appears when you position the mouse pointer over the photo (see Figure 5-5). The navigation bar disappears when you move the pointer off the image so that you can get the full effect of the slide show. Click Play, and the photos appear one by one, with no further interaction from you. Sit back and enjoy!

Figure 5-4: Click the down arrow on the right side of the photo album to choose the view you want.

Figure 5-5: Select Full View to display your photo album in the Photo tab.

Montage view is a great effect in MSN Spaces. This view enables you to see all your photos in a particular album as a colorful collection of your favorite images—in miniature size. You can display Montage view on your space's page as part of the photo album—so that instead of your photo album rotating images one by one, as in Slideshow view, your favorite photos appear as thumbnails, with individual photos enlarging over the rest in a random pattern or when a viewer "hovers" the mouse over the image (see Figure 5-6). This is a beautiful and fun effect, sure to wow the friends and family who visit your space.

Figure 5-6: Montage view displays all the photos in your album as thumbnail images—click the one you want to see up close.

Photo Blogging

Now that you know what to do with the collections of photos you want to share, what about those times when you want to add a photo to illustrate the story you're telling in your blog? (If you're not sure what a blog is or what you might do with one, refer to Chapter 4, "Adding and Editing Blog Entries," to find out what you're missing!) When you add a blog entry about your new car, about the wild skate-boarding event you went to last weekend, or about the home-and-garden show where your prized azalea won a blue ribbon, you'll want to add a photo to show friends and family what you're talking about. The process is simple:

1. Click Edit Your Space; then in the Blog area, click Add Entry.

2. Enter the title as usual, and type the text that tells the story. Use the format-ting controls to make the text look the way you want it to look.

③ Now click Add Photos at the bottom of the blog entry window (see Figure 5-7).

④ Using the folder list in the left panel of the Add Photos window, navigate to the folder containing the photo(s) you want to add.

⑤ Click the checkbox in the upper-left corner of a photo to select it. Select any additional photos you want to include as part of this blog entry.

⑥ Click Upload Now to add the selected photo(s) to your blog.

The photo name appears at the bottom of the blog entry window.

⑦ Click Publish Entry to add the entry and photo to your blog.

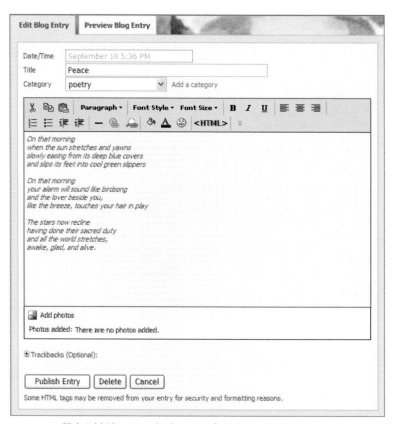

Figure 5-7: Click Add Photos at the bottom of the blog entry window to attach a photo.

Once the photo is added to your blog, it appears as a small thumbnail image at the end of the text (see Figure 5-8). Visitors can display the photo in a full window by clicking it. MSN Spaces automatically creates a new photo album called My Blog Photos in which all photos added to your blog entries are stored. You can view the My Blog Photos album by clicking it in the album list.

If your cell phone contains a digital camera, you can post your photos remotely by e-mailing your photos to an address unique to your MSN Spaces account. For more information on setting up your space for mobile blogging, see Chapter 2, "Getting a Space of Your Own."

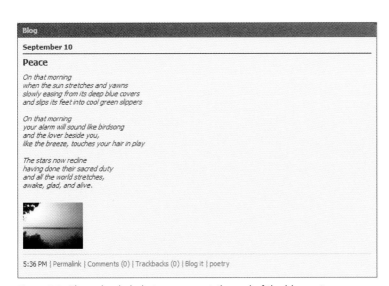

Figure 5-8: The uploaded photo appears at the end of the blog entry.

Editing Your Photos

One of the great features of working with MSN Spaces is that it's convenient—you can tell your story and add your photos quickly, with a minimum of time and hassle. But what if the photo you just took on your cell phone is a bit too dark? Instead of taking the time to open your image-editing program, edit the photo, and then upload it to MSN Spaces, you can perform the editing just before you upload it to your space, using the MSN Spaces image-editing tools.

Here's the process to follow when you want to edit a photo you're about to upload:

① Click Edit Your Space to change to Edit mode on your space.

② In the Photo Album area, click Create (if you're creating a new album) or Edit (if you're adding photos to an album you've already created).

③ In the Create Album or Edit Album window, click Add Photos. The Add Photos dialog box appears.

④ Click the photo you want to edit; then click Edit Photos. The photo displays in the editing window, and a new toolbar of editing tools appears across the top of the work area (see Figure 5-9).

Figure 5-9: MSN Spaces includes image-editing tools that you can use to improve your photos before you display them in your space.

⑤ Edit the selected photo by simply clicking the tool you want to use. Here's a quick overview of what the various tools do:

- Previous and Next select the preceding or following photo in the images you selected for editing.

- Zoom In and Zoom Out enlarge or reduce the size of the displayed image.

- Rotate Clockwise and Rotate Counter-Clockwise turn the photo 90 degrees to the right or left.

- Increase Brightness and Decrease Brightness enable you to change the lighting in your photo.

- Crop enables you to reduce the image to the most important part.

- Reset returns the photo to its original, unedited state.

⑥ When the photo looks the way you want it, click Upload Now to add the photo to your photo album (or blog entry).

Click View Thumbnails to return the display to the complete collection of photos for the selected album.

TIP

ORGANIZING YOUR PHOTOS

MSN Spaces gives you a whopping amount of storage space for your favorite photos, but you may be surprised to see how quickly that space fills up! To make the most of the space you have available, it's important to keep photos organized. Here are a few tips to help you keep your photo operation running smoothly:

- Create separate albums for different photo topics.

- Give photos descriptive names that will function as short captions. (The filenames will appear in Slideshow view and Full view.)

- Update and discard old photos regularly. (For example, whenever you add new images, look for ones you can remove to save space.)

DELETING PHOTOS

When you're ready to delete some of the photos you've used on your space, click Edit Your Space, select the photo album you want, and click Edit. The photos in the album you selected display as thumbnails in the Edit Album window. Select the photo you want to delete, and then either press the Delete key or click Delete Selected Photos. MSN Spaces will ask you to confirm that you want to delete the photo; click Yes to finish the process.

You can also delete photos you no longer need by clicking Edit Your Space and then clicking Settings. Now click the Storage tab at the top of the space area. A list of photos in the selected photo album appears (see Figure 5-10). Click the checkboxes of the photos you'd like to delete, and click the Delete button at the bottom of the list.

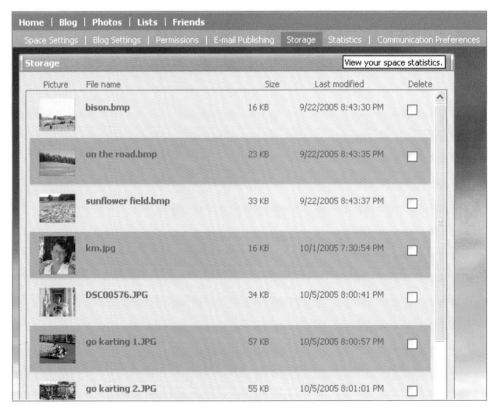

Figure 5-10: Select the photo you want to delete, and then click Delete; when MSN Spaces asks you to confirm, click Yes or press Enter.

RENAMING PHOTOS

Renaming photos is simple. Anytime a photo is displayed in the Edit Album window or the Add Photos window, you can change the name of the photo by clicking the existing name and typing a new name in the textbox that appears (see Figure 5-11). MSN Spaces then saves the new name with no further action from you. Sweet.

Figure 5-11: Rename a photo by simply clicking the existing file-name and typing a new one.

Get Everyone Involved with Photo Comments

If people are just coming to your space and then leaving, that's only half the fun you could be having. MSN Spaces version 2 includes a terrific photo commenting feature that enables your friends and family to add their own captions, comments, and quips to the photos you post. Each photo can have its own comments, which radically increases the interaction you can have in your space!

Here's how it might work: Suppose you recently participated in a fundraising marathon for a worthy cause. Your friends from work regularly visit your space to see what you're writing about, learn about your training, and add notes to encourage and challenge you. You have posted a series of photos about your last trip to the gym—ones where the weights are practically pinning you to the bench—and your friends are having a good time ribbing you about it by adding comments to your photos. (Don't worry—you'll get a chance to comment on *their* spaces, too!)

The photo comments feature, similar to the commenting feature available for blog entries, enables others to log in and add their own notes and ideas to your photos. Comments, along with descriptions (a feature you can use to provide a longer text description of an individual photo), appear in the Details pane at the bottom of the photo album (see Figure 5-12).

Figure 5-12: Photo comments invite viewers to add their own thoughts about the photos you post.

To add a comment to a space, viewers simply click Add A Comment. The Add A Comment window opens in the Details pane. Your friends add their name and type the comment they want to leave; then they click Publish Comment to save the comment with the image. Don't take their ribbing too much to heart—you'll be the one in shape the next time swimsuit season rolls around! Also, remember to visit the spaces of the people who add comments on your space. In addition to those who already stop by, you may wind up with a huge network of new friends, all fellow space makers!

TIP

If you want to turn off comments on your space so people won't be able to comment on your blog entries and photos, click Edit Your Space, and click Blog Settings. In the Comments area, uncheck the Allow Comments box. Scroll down to the bottom of the page, and click Save to finalize your changes.

FOUR SIMPLE TIPS FOR GREAT PHOTOS

Taking good photographs is a lot like learning any new skill—the more you do it, the better you'll get. As you add photos to your space, use these basic ideas to help make your photos the best they can be:

Go for impact   The best photos have some kind of emotional appeal—happy faces, beautiful spaces, nostalgic images of childhood. Be aware of what makes you say "Oooh!" and "Aaah!" Remember that those visiting your space are likely to feel a similar connection to the images you display.

Crop to the best part   It's a common mistake, but we often use whole photos on sites, reports, and documents when just a portion of the image would be more effective. For example, suppose you have a photo of your cousin sky-diving, but in addition to the plane, you have captured the whole landscape—as well as a nearby mountain—in the same shot. You can crop the photo to only the plane, your cousin, and the blue sky behind her to get the most impact from a single image.

Be bright and fresh   Touching up the brightness and color in a photo takes just a minute or two and can make a great difference in the overall impact of a photo. Most image editors have brightness and color controls that are easy to use; some programs, such as Microsoft Picture Manager (available with Microsoft Office 2003), include automatic correction features that will make the adjustments for you.

Show faces and places and fun   We know that the human eye is naturally drawn to images of faces. Places of beauty also capture our attention and imagination. If you want to inspire the people who visit your space, show them something interesting and fun. Give them a picture they want to imagine themselves in!

Sharing Lists of Songs, Books, and More

CHAPTER 6

People all over the planet use lists every day to keep track of all sorts of items—grocery lists, to-do lists, and bills to pay are just a few examples. Creating lists is one of the simplest ways to organize all kinds of information, which is probably why it's so popular all over the world. Listing tasks isn't something that's necessarily taught to us; it's just something we do.

People all over the planet use lists every day to keep track of all sorts of items.

Lists aren't only ubiquitous in "everyday life"—they're also scattered all over the Web and your PC. Your files appear as lists in Microsoft Windows, your Start menu is a list of available programs, and Google search results display as a list of hyperlinks. David Letterman has even made a (great) living from silly lists such as "Top 10 Questions to Ask Yourself Before Eating a 15-Pound Cheeseburger." Lists are absolutely *everywhere*.

Since you can use lists for just about anything, creating lists and sharing them are great ways to communicate and tell people more about you: Who are you? What do you like and dislike? What kind of music do you listen to most often? What are your New Year's resolutions? Lists are incredibly flexible, so it's only natural that MSN Spaces makes it possible to create, manage, and share lists on your space!

Various Types of Lists

MSN Spaces makes your life a little easier by getting you started with a few special list types: a music list, book list, and blog list. Each type is slightly different and is geared toward the type of information you'll be placing on the list. For example, if you're adding a song to a music list, you might want to also add album and artist information. This kind of functionality, while great for songs, wouldn't work as well for your list of favorite blogs. The information you probably want to share in your music playlists is pretty specific to your music, so the music list type is considered special. Thanks to these simple list types, you're able to add detailed lists to your space without much effort.

But the fun certainly doesn't stop there. One of the best features of lists in MSN Spaces is that they can become just about anything you need them to be. Sure, a few special types of lists are available that you can create easily, but you can also "break the mold" and use lists in your own unique ways. When you start to think of all the topics people keep in lists, you can probably see how the possibilities are virtually limitless!

Spicing Up Your Space with Tunes

Music on the Internet has officially arrived. The rise of digital music players (such as the Apple iPod or the Creative Zen Micro) and the dozens of online music stores have turned digital music into a reality. People using music to express themselves isn't new; it has been going on since the first cave dweller learned how to whistle. However, never before has it been so easy!

With MSN Spaces, not only can you share your music playlists with your visitors, but you can do so in just a couple of clicks. You don't have to spend thousands of grueling hours entering information from CD sleeves. If you use Windows Media Player, you can share any playlist you've already created (including auto-playlists such as "Five Star Favorites") on your space without any extra effort on your part (see the "Copying a Playlist from Windows Media Player" section).

> It's important to point out that what is actually being shared on your space is the information (or *metadata*) associated with your music, not the music itself. Your visitors will see the name of the album, artist, and song—but they will not be able to copy the song from your hard drive or from MSN Spaces. MSN Spaces doesn't let you share the music itself because most music is protected by copyright, and sharing the music without permission is a violation of copyright.
>
> NOTE

If you don't use Windows Media Player but still want to share your music tastes with your friends and family, you can do so just by typing in song information.

CREATING A MUSIC LIST

Creating a music list on your space consists of two simple steps: naming the list and adding a song to it. To create a music list from scratch, just follow these steps:

1. From Edit mode of your space, click the Music tab at the top of the page. (If you don't see the Music tab, this means you don't currently have the Music module in your space. See Chapter 7, "Your Space, Your Way," to learn how to add and remove modules.) This will display all the music lists currently shared on your space. The page should be empty unless you've already added one or more lists on your own (see Figure 6-1).

2. Click Add Music List under Music Tasks to create a new music list.

> **NOTE**
> You can create a maximum of 25 music lists on your space, and each music list can have up to 100 songs.

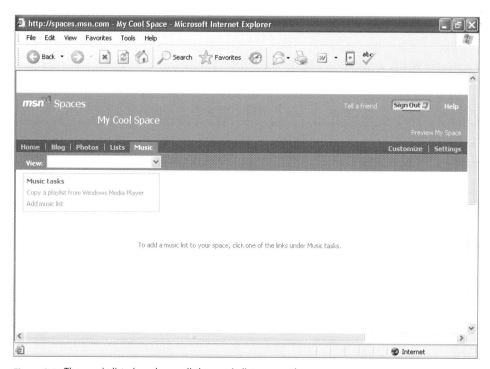

Figure 6-1: The music list view shows all the music lists currently on your space.

③ Give your music list a name, and click OK.

This is a required step; if you cancel at this point, your music list won't be created.

Once you've added your music list, the list will be displayed automatically—and it will be added to the View drop-down list at the top of the page.

④ Click Add Song. Immediately, three boxes will appear: Song Name (Required), Artist Name, and Album Name (see Figure 6-2). Fill in the boxes with your song information.

⑤ Click Add to add the song to the music list.

When you're ready to add more songs to the list, you can just repeat steps 4 and 5. Quick tip: although the edit boxes for each new song are displayed at the top of the current list, each new song is actually added to the bottom of the list.

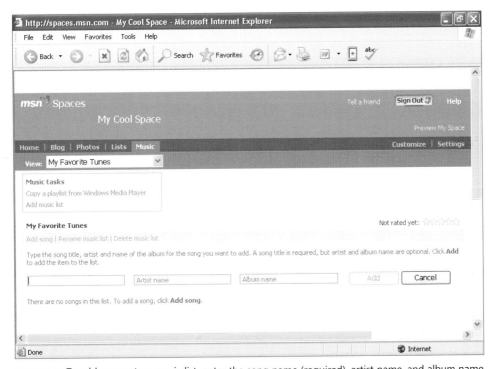

Figure 6-2: To add a song to a music list, enter the song name (required), artist name, and album name.

TIP

As soon as you create your music list, it's automatically available on your MSN Spaces home page for visitors to see. If you'd like to choose where the music list appears on the page, you'll need to enter Edit mode and then click Customize to move it. (See Chapter 7, "Your Space, Your Way," for more information on layout and customization.)

REMOVING AND EDITING SONGS

What happens if you made a spelling error and want to correct it? Simple. All you have to do is click the Edit icon (pencil) to the right of the song details, and edit boxes immediately appear. Enter your changes, and click Save. Your changes will then be saved to your list. Clicking Cancel will make the edit boxes disappear again, and your changes will not be applied.

If you want to remove a song, all you have to do is click the Delete icon (black *X*) to the right of the Edit icon. You'll be asked if you're sure (see Figure 6-3). If you are, click OK, and *voilà!*—no more song. You can always click Cancel at this point if you've changed your mind and want to keep the song.

COPYING A PLAYLIST FROM WINDOWS MEDIA PLAYER

Windows Media Player is a program included with most versions of Microsoft Windows for listening to music and watching DVDs and videos. MSN Spaces makes the act of adding music information as simple as uploading your existing playlists from Windows Media Player directly to your space! This is especially handy if you're a weekend DJ and create lots of playlists.

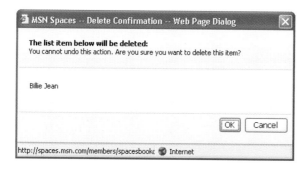

Figure 6-3: To remove a song from a music list, you must first say it's OK.

If you aren't familiar with playlists, they're just named collections of songs (such as "Driving Music"); you can create them by adding songs manually or automatically based on song characteristics (album name, tempo, rating, and so on). Playlists in Windows Media Player are pretty similar in nature to the old "mix tapes" of the 1980s and 1990s...or the list of songs queued up to play from the table jukebox at your favorite 24-hour diner.

> Importing songs from Windows Media Player will work only with Internet Explorer 6 or later and Windows Media Player version 9 or later. (The latest version of Windows Media Player at the time of this printing is version 10.) If you don't already have Windows Media Player 10 on your system, you can download it for free from Microsoft at http://www.microsoft.com/windows/windowsmedia/. To download the most recent version of Internet Explorer for free from Microsoft, visit http://www.microsoft.com/ie.
>
> NOTE

To import a playlist from Windows Media Player, follow these steps:

1. From Edit mode of your space, click the Music tab at the top of the page. This will display all the music lists currently shared on your space.

2. Click Copy A Playlist from Windows Media Player under Music Tasks to import a playlist into your space.

3. You'll be presented with a dialog box for security asking whether you'd like to grant "read access" to your music library (see Figure 6-4). In plain English, this is MSN Spaces asking for permission to examine your media library. Windows Media Player is configured to ask you first because it's accessing personal files stored on your hard drive. If you're OK with this, click Yes. Otherwise, click No.

Figure 6-4: To respect your privacy, MSN Spaces first asks whether it can access your playlists.

④ If you have a large music library, you may encounter a delay while MSN Spaces reads your playlists from Windows Media Player.

Once it's finished, all your playlists (including auto-playlists such as "Fresh Tracks") will appear on the page for you to select.

⑤ Once your playlists are on the screen, you can see which songs are in each playlist by clicking the plus/minus sign next to its name. When you're ready to choose a playlist, select the button next to the name, and click Next to continue. (Again, if your playlist is large, you may see a delay!)

⑥ On the next (and final) page, you can unselect the songs from the playlist that you don't want to copy to your space. By default, all songs will be selected. Once you're ready, click Copy to start the copy.

⑦ Once your music information is copied, you'll see all the songs listed on the page (see Figure 6-5). At this point, you can edit the list items manually, delete them, or add new songs to the list if you want.

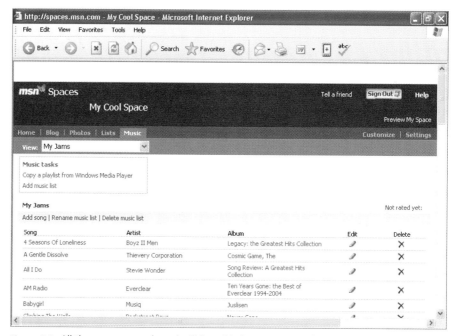

Figure 6-5: All the songs you selected will be added to your music list automatically—artist and album name included!

RATING PLAYLISTS

Music tastes tend to be controversial no matter what they are. Justin Timberlake fans don't always relate to Miles Davis fans, and those screaming teens at Mariah Carey concerts may not always understand the appeal of Simon and Garfunkel. Part of this is probably because music tastes are personal and expressive. Case in point: dozens of online surveys map your music tastes to your personality. In sum, not all music lovers love the same music.

Along these lines, MSN Spaces gives you a way to "vote" for the music lists you like with a five-star rating system. This rating is associated with the music list as an average. So, if you find a music list within MSN Spaces you'd like to rate—good or bad— just click one of the stars next to the name of the list. Five stars indicates a great list, while one star is a poor one.

You'll get a confirmation dialog box before your rating is recorded. Just like everything else, clicking OK will save your rating and Cancel will cancel it.

USING THE MSN MUSIC CONNECTION

MSN Music is Microsoft's digital warehouse of online music. People can buy individual songs or entire albums from MSN and download them to their PC. One of the hidden benefits of using the built-in music list feature in MSN Spaces is that it automatically links your songs with the MSN Music store at http://music.msn.com.

The MSN Music store has a large selection of music. When someone clicks music in any of your music lists, they will be taken to that song within the MSN Music store. At that point, they can preview the song or buy/download the song. They can even play music videos or read reviews of the artists and albums they have selected.

How does this work exactly? When you enter information into your music lists (either by typing it in or copying it from Windows Media Player), MSN Spaces stores this information for you. When someone visits your space and clicks one of your songs, MSN Spaces sends a search query to the MSN Music store with your information. MSN Music makes its best educated guess based on the album, song, or artist information and looks up the information in its database of music. If the song is available from MSN Music, your visitors will be taken directly to that artist, album, and song to explore!

LINKING TO OTHER MUSIC STORES

Although MSN Spaces automatically links your music to the MSN Music store, it's also possible to create lists of music that link to an alternative music store. Although this isn't a supported feature and takes a little bit of work, you can do this if you're determined enough. However, this has some downsides. You don't get to use all the features specific to music lists, namely, ratings and the music-specific fields such as Artist and Album. The list will also appear on its own on your space; it won't be grouped with the rest of your music. If none of this is important to you, keep reading.

To link to other music stores, you'll first need to create a custom list (see the "Getting Creative with Custom Lists" section for information on how to do this). The title and description can be whatever you want—you can use the title for the song name and the description for the album name or a short description of the song. In the URL field, you need to fill in the Web address for that song on your favorite music store.

The following are the uniform resource locators (URLs) to use for some of the most popular music stores.

ITUNES MUSIC STORE

Apple hosts a Web page (http://www.apple.com/itunes/linkmaker/) that makes linking to songs on iTunes a cinch. You just enter the song, album, and artist name, and Apple gives you the exact URL to use. Just copy and paste the "itms://" URL directly into the URL field in your custom list!

YAHOO MUSIC

To link to music on Yahoo Music, visit http://music.yahoo.com in your Web browser, and search for the song or album to which you're interested in linking. Once you've found it, copy and paste the URL from your browser's address bar into the URL field for your list item.

Alternatively, you could construct a URL by hand if you're adventurous. To do this, you'll have to understand a bit about how URLs work. Most important, you need to replace spaces with plus (+) signs since spaces aren't valid within a URL. The following is a link to Dave Matthews in Yahoo Music:

http://search.music.yahoo.com/launch/search/?m=all&p=dave+matthews

To replace Dave Matthews with Cowboy Troy, you just need to replace everything after "p=" in the URL. This is what the URL would look like for Cowboy Troy:

http://search.music.yahoo.com/launch/search/?m=all&p=cowboy+troy

AMAZON

To link to music on Amazon, first find the album you'd like to link to by searching or browsing from Amazon's home page at http://www.amazon.com. Once you land on the page you'd like to link to, simply copy and paste the URL from your browser's address bar into the URL field for your list item.

An easier way to do this is to use the Amazon Associates link builder. To use the link builder, you'll need to sign up for an Amazon Associate ID and log in to Amazon Associates Central at http://associates.amazon.com.

Ready for the Book Club: Listing Books

One of the most popular uses of lists is for books—all you need to do is provide the name of the book.

CREATING A BOOK LIST

To create a book list, follow these steps:

1. From Edit mode of your space, click the Lists tab at the top of the page. This will display all the lists currently shared on your space.

2. Click Create A List under List Tasks to start a new book list.

3. Give your list a name, and select Book List in the drop-down below the title. Click OK to continue. This is a required step; if you cancel at this point, your book list won't be created.

   Once you've added your book list, you're now viewing that list. You can tell because the list is automatically selected in the View drop-down at the top of the page containing all your lists.

④ Click Add Item. Immediately, five boxes will appear: Title (Required), Author, Description, ISBN (International Standard Book Number), and URL. Fill in the boxes with your book's information.

⑤ Click Add to add the book to the list, and it will show up immediately.

Creating a List of Your Favorite Blogs

One of the most interesting aspects of the "blogosphere" is the way it's distributed across the Internet is still very connected. The way connections are made is through the standard hyperlink, something that has been around since the inception of the World Wide Web in the early 1990s.

In the blogging world, these connections are incredibly important because they form a "social fabric" that connects people to other people, not just pages to pages. People use their *blogroll* (a collection of links to other weblogs) as a way to tell others whose blogs they read, who they know, and even who they have dated in the past. Just like everything else on MSN Spaces, you can use your blog list however you want. It could be a standard blogroll of interesting blogs or spaces, or it could be a list of links to the RSS feeds you read. (You can read more about RSS in Appendix A, "RSS Q&A: Interview with an RSS Aficionado.")

To create your blog list, follow these steps:

① From Edit mode of your space, click the Lists tab at the top of the page. This will display all the lists currently shared on your space.

② Click Create A List under List Tasks to start a new blog list.

③ Give your list a name, and select Blog List in the drop-down list below the title. Click OK to continue.

This is a required step; if you cancel at this point, your blog list won't be created.

Once you've added your blog list, you're now viewing that list. You can tell because the list is automatically selected in the View drop-down list at the top of the page containing all your lists.

④ Click Add Item. Immediately, three boxes will appear: Name (Required), URL, and Description. Fill in the boxes with your information.

⑤ Click Add to add the blog to the list. It will then be added automatically to the list.

Simply rinse and repeat step 4 to add more people to this blog list. If you'd like to start another blog list, you can just repeat all the previous steps. This is useful if you want to separate your blog list in some way. For example, you could separate them as "Blogs I Read Daily" and "Blogs I Read Weekly."

LINKING TO A BLOGROLL

If you use Bloglines (http://www.bloglines.com), NewsGator Online (http://www .newsgator.com), or any other online service that supports sharing your blogroll on a Web page, you can easily link to it from an MSN Spaces list. You'll need to create a custom list (you may want to call it "My Blogroll") and add just one item to the list, pointing the item to your service.

For example, to link to your blogroll on Bloglines, you'll first need to make your blogroll public. To do this, log in to your Bloglines account (http://www.bloglines .com), and click Options and then Blog Settings. On this page, enter a username, and select Yes, Publish My Blog And/Or Blogroll. Once you save your changes by clicking OK, your blogroll will be available to anyone with the URL. (Your URL will be http://www.bloglines.com/public/<your username>.) Now you just need to type your URL into your list item to share it via your space.

IMPORTING A BLOGROLL

MSN Spaces doesn't support importing a blogroll from another service, but some enterprising software developers have provided a way to do it. A Web page, created by an MSN developer, Ines Khelifi, reads an OPML file from the Web (more on that in a minute) and outputs your blogroll ready for you to copy and paste into a blog post. Once you've done this, you can add the Permalink URL of your new blog post to a list, and you have an instant blogroll. For more on Permalinks and how they relate to blogging, see Chapter 4, "Adding and Editing Blog Entries."

You can find this tool at http://www.inesk.net/Tools/RSS_Reader.aspx.

OPML is the Outline Processor Markup Language, a document format used primarily for blogrolls. NewsGator, Bloglines, RSS Bandit, and just about every other RSS reader supports importing and exporting OPML.

Getting Creative with Custom Lists

With custom lists, you're able to create lists of virtually anything you can imagine. A quick scan of some spaces reveals some fun uses of lists:

- Home improvement list

- Weekend to-do list

- Upcoming concerts

- Favorite drinks at Starbucks

- What's in my purse right now

- Top ten life events

- Favorite TV shows (see Figure 6-6)

Custom lists consist of just three input fields: Title, URL, and Description. The lists are always displayed the same way with the title automatically hyperlinked to the URL above the description, all within the overall theme for the space.

Figure 6-6: Favorite TV shows are just one example of a custom list.

CREATING A CUSTOM LIST

To create your custom list, follow these steps:

1. From Edit mode of your space, click the Lists tab at the top of the page. This will display all the lists currently shared on your space.

2. Click Create A List under List Tasks to start a new list.

3. Give your list a name, and select Custom List in the drop-down list below the title. Click OK to continue.

   This is a required step; if you cancel at this point, your list won't be created.

   Once you've added your list, you're now viewing that list. You can tell because the list is automatically selected in the View drop-down at the top of the page containing all your lists.

4. Click Add Item. Immediately, three boxes will appear: Name (Required), URL, and Description. Fill in the boxes with your information.

5. Click Add to add an item to the list.

So now that you know how to create any type of list, let's get creative and explore some list options!

ANNOUNCEMENTS

Lists don't necessarily have to consist of more than one list item. People also use lists as a way to display announcements, disclaimers, and copyright statements on their spaces. To add an announcement to your space, first create a custom list called "Announcement." Add your announcement text to a list item in the Name or Description field; you don't need to enter a URL unless you want to link to another Web page. Note that these fields are limited to just a few lines of text—you can't write a novel here!

You can now place your announcement wherever you want to make sure people don't miss it. See Chapter 7, "Your Space, Your Way," for more information on layout and customization.

FAVORITE THINGS

You can use custom lists to share your favorite Web sites, movies, TV shows, locations—whatever! One of the fun parts about doing this is linking your favorites to Web sites representing those topics.

For example, you could add a link to the "CSI" Web site—or your favorite fan site—from your "My Favorite Shows" list. You could link to an online map or satellite image on MSN Virtual Earth or Yahoo Maps when listing your favorite coffee shops. Or you could link directly to the Apple QuickTime trailer of your favorite movie from your movie list so your friends can see what you're so excited about!

WISH LIST

Tired of being asked what you want for your birthday every year? Keep a running list of those gift ideas on your space by linking directly to items in online stores such as Amazon or Buy.com. You can even sort the items by priority so there's no guessing come that special day.

If you already have a wish list somewhere, just link directly to it!

ITEMS YOU'RE SELLING

Looking to get rid of that old, beat-up, red couch? Use MSN Spaces as a classifieds ad to alert your friends, family, or strangers of merchandise you're selling. Thanks to the integration of MSN Spaces in places such as MSN Hotmail and MSN Messenger, people will know immediately that you have something for sale.

You have a couple of ways to do this with lists:

1. Create a custom list ("Items for Sale"), and list each item as an individual entry.

   This works but might be a bit tedious to update when you sell something or change the price. Instead, you could link each list item directly to the item's page on eBay or Amazon auctions.

or

1. Be lazy, and link directly to your eBay or Amazon member profile, listing all the items you have for sale on either of those services.

HOT TOPICS

A Hot Topics list is a collection of links to previous blog entries, making it easy for visitors to find them when they land on your space.

If you're an active blogger, you're going to have posts that have a little bit (or a lot) more significance than others. If you'd like to make sure those posts are easily accessible from your space, the easiest way to do this is to create a list of links to those entries!

"SUBSCRIBE WITH" LINKS

Many people using MSN Spaces are doing so to make it possible for friends, family, and even strangers to stay connected to them. One way people can do this is through RSS readers or portal pages such as My MSN or My Yahoo. (See Appendix A, "RSS Q&A: Interview with an RSS Aficionado," for more details.)

Creating a list so people can subscribe in different ways is a great method to keep people connected to you. If you're interested in providing easy ways for people to add your space to RSS readers or portal pages, create a list with the following URLs. Make sure to insert your MSN Spaces username where it says <username>.

MyMSN   http://my.msn.com/addtomymsn.armx?id=rss&ut=http://spaces .msn.com/<username>&ru=http://spaces.msn.com/<username >/feed.rss

My Yahoo   http://add.my.yahoo.com/rss?url=http://spaces.msn.com/ <username>/feed.rss

Bloglines   http://www.bloglines.com/sub/http://spaces.msn.com/<username>/ feed.rss

NewsGator Online   http://www.newsgator.com/ngs/subscriber/subext.aspx? url=http://spaces.msn.com/<username>/feed.rss

Desktop aggregators (FeedDemon, RSS Bandit, NetNewsWire, and Others)   feed://spaces.msn.com/<username>/feed.rss

LANGUAGE TRANSLATION

One of the greatest attributes of the Internet is its diversity. MSN Spaces is available in more than 15 languages in 30 international markets—but that doesn't mean much if the language you're writing in isn't the one your visitor can read. Fret not! There is a roundabout solution to this: using an online translation service to translate your words.

NOTE

With translation services, you're likely to get a clumsy but comprehensible rendering in the target language at best, but often you'll get a severely garbled version. As a reality check, put part of the translated version back through the translation engine to see what resemblance it bears to your original.

First, create a custom list called "Translate This Space." Next, add the translation links using Google Language Tools by following these steps:

1. Visit http://www.google.com/language_tools, and enter your MSN Spaces URL under Translate A Web Page.

2. Choose a language conversion (for example, English to Spanish), and click Translate.

3. Copy and paste the resulting URL from your browser's address bar into a new item in your custom list (for example, "Read This in Spanish").

4. Repeat for every language into which you want your space translated!

GUEST BOOK

One of the missing features in MSN Spaces is the ability to leave a comment on a space itself. Comments on blog entries and photo albums are commonplace, but many times people just want to say hello—or they want to comment on your space, not necessarily on something you've said or photographs you've taken.

The easiest way to enable a guest book in MSN Spaces is to create a blog entry titled "Guest Book." The content of the entry could just contain something like this:

Leave a comment below to sign my guest book!

After you post this entry, it will appear as a standard blog entry. Now, create a custom list called "My Guest Book," and add just one entry to the list called "Leave a Comment!" The URL of this list item should be the Permalink of the blog entry you just posted to your space. Now you have a guest book!

OTHER IDEAS

Here are some other fun ideas for lists:

- Your favorite MSN Groups
- E-mail links to send an email message (these look like mailto://email @address.com, where "email@address.com" is the actual e-mail address)
- Your own top ten lists
- Timelines/key dates for projects
- Your goals
- Famous quotes and wise words
- Links to posts on other spaces
- Copyright statements and disclaimers
- Your favorite charities

EDITING OR REMOVING A LIST ITEM

Editing or removing list items from a blog, book, or custom list is the same as removing a song from a music list. To edit a list item, click the Edit icon (pencil) next to the entry in the list. And to remove a list item, click the Delete icon (black *X*) next to the entry in the list (see Figure 6-7).

Once you've created a list, it's pretty natural to want to sort the list in a particular order. Unfortunately, MSN Spaces doesn't provide an easy way to do this just yet. In the meantime, here's what you need to do: From Edit mode of your space, click the Lists tab at the top of the page. Select the list in the Lists drop-down list that contains the items you'd like to sort. Click the Edit icon of the list item you'd like at the bottom of the list, and then click Save (you don't have to change any of the content). When you refresh the page, the item you just edited will be at the bottom of the list. You can do this as many times as you want until you get the list in the right order. It's a little tedious, but it works!

TIP

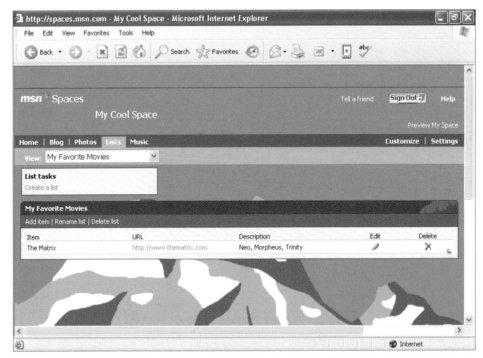

Figure 6-7: To edit a list item within a list, click the Edit icon (the pencil); to remove an item, click the Delete icon (the black X).

RENAMING AND DELETING LISTS

What if the songs on your "Favorite Songs" list are no longer your favorites? Simple, all you have to do is rename the list to something like "My Old Favorite Songs." Or you can remove the list completely. To rename any list, follow these steps:

1. If the list you'd like to rename is a book, blog, or custom list, click the Lists tab to view your lists, and then select the list you'd like to rename in the View drop-down list. If the list is a music list, click the Music tab, and select the specific music list.

2. Click the Rename List or Rename Music List link underneath the list you'd like to rename.

3. Give your list a new name, and click OK. (Pick something fun!) If you click Cancel, your old name remains.

To delete a list, follow these steps:

1. Select the list you'd like to delete in the View drop-down list.

2. Click the Delete List or Delete Music List link underneath the title of the list you'd like to delete.

3. If you're sure you'd like to delete the list, click OK. You can't get the list back, so make sure this is what you want to do! If you want to meditate on it for a bit, click Cancel (see Figure 6-8).

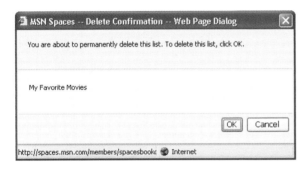

MSN Spaces -- Delete Confirmation -- Web Page Dialog

You are about to permanently delete this list. To delete this list, click OK.

My Favorite Movies

[OK] [Cancel]

http://spaces.msn.com/members/spacesbook   Internet

Figure 6-8: Once a list is removed, it's lost forever; clicking Cancel will keep the list on your space.

Your Space, Your Way

CHAPTER 7

One of the great features of creating a space of your own is that it is all yours—you can do whatever you want with it. Express yourself! Post your favorite photos. Tell your stories. List your favorite tunes. Talk about the books you've read lately, the great place you went to dinner, or the cute stuff the kids said or did today.

The customization features of MSN Spaces make it easy for you to personalize the look and feel of your space so that it reflects your personality and displays the style you want.

In addition to being able to express yourself the way you want, the customization features of MSN Spaces make it easy for you to personalize the look and feel of your space so that it reflects your personality and displays the style you want. You can choose a theme that is artsy, friendly, or professional; rearrange your layout so the features you enjoy most get the majority of space on your page; and even add a special image as your background.

Customizing Your Space

By now you know that whenever you want to update your space, you start by clicking Edit Your Space in the upper-right corner of your space. Then you click Customize on the same side of the screen. A new bar of options appears, giving you the following four choices:

Themes   Click this when you want to choose a new theme for your space.

Modules   Click this when you're interested in changing the items that appear on your space—the lists, photo album, profile, and more.

Layout   Click this when you want to change the way all the elements on your space are arranged.

Background   Click this when you want to use your own photo in place of the background used on your space. (Or, if you've already tried that and want to return to the default background, use this option to do that.)

CHOOSING A NEW THEME

The theme of your space is the overall design—it includes the background colors and images (for example, the beautiful snowflake or cute puppies that are part of the background page); all the colors used for list boxes (called *modules*), title bars, menu bars, and more; and the color of all text (the text you type and the text that appears as menu options, links, and more). The theme you choose for your space is really important because it has everything to do with how your readers view your space. Is it hard to read? Is the design welcoming and fun? Do people *like* being there? Each of these questions has something to do with the experience you create for your space visitors—and that experience is directly related to the theme you choose for your space.

MSN Spaces includes a huge palette of theme possibilities, so you're sure to find a style that fits the personality you want to portray on your space. To see what kinds of themes are available, begin in Edit mode, click Customize, and then click Themes. The Themes drop-down list opens (see Figure 7-1). At the top of the list, you'll see a palette of six featured themes; beneath the featured themes, you'll see various theme categories. Click a category you want see, and theme examples appear in a submenu. Click the theme you'd like to apply to your space, or click the submenu a second time to close it.

If you want to see all the themes presented side by side instead of browsing through the categories, scroll to the bottom of the Themes list, and select View All.

TIP

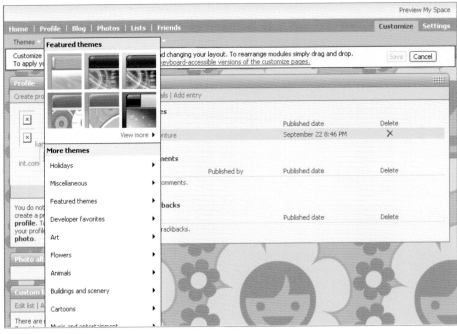

Figure 7-1: Choose a new theme to change the personality of your space.

Figure 7-2 shows a space with a theme selected from the Nature category. Notice that the theme contains a wide range of colors that all work together—from the background image to the menu bar and options, text, title, and more.

NOTE The theme you select will also be applied to your contact card. Not familiar with contact cards? This is what appears to MSN Messenger users when they click the "gleam" next to your member name in their MSN Messenger windows. The gleam tells them you've updated your space. When they click the gleam, the contact card opens, displaying your MSN Messenger info and showing the title of your most recent post as well as mini-thumbnails of the last several photos you've uploaded. Pretty slick! See Chapter 8, "Connecting Spaces and Creating Community," for additional details.

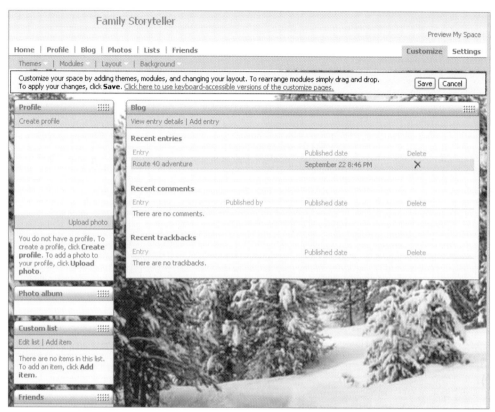

Figure 7-2: Trying a new theme is like painting a room a fresh color—it can add life and excitement to your space.

CHOOSING YOUR MODULES

Once you find a theme you like, you may want make some changes in the types of items that are displayed on your space. MSN Spaces calls the different items *modules*—and when you first create your space, the Profile, Blog, Photo Album, Custom List, Friends, Category, Archives, and Updates Spaces modules appear by default. The Modules option enables you to make choices about which modules are used and where they appear on your space. Begin the process in Edit mode by clicking Customize if necessary.

MSN BACKSTORY: **WHAT'S IN A THEME?**

The following blog entry, used with permission from **Karen Luk**'s space (http://www.spaces.msn.com/members/k/), illustrates the advantages of using predesigned themes:

So I've been working with a number of designers over the last couple of releases to do theming—as you can see with the themes, some are super simple, and others are actually kind of complex with lots of colors.

Just by looking at them, themes don't seem *that* complicated—what's picking a few colors? Well, it's plenty hard to do, trust me. I made those really plain themes (blue, red, green, black) that a number of people have said are ugly and a number of people have written in to thank me for "a plain theme without those stupid-looking corners." Those themes literally had five colors. I can pick five colors that match, especially when two of them are black and white!

But, if you've tried the PowerToy for tweaking colors on your space, you might have found that picking colors isn't as simple as it first seems (not to mention that the PowerToy is for power users who know what hex (hexadecimal) codes are and how they work). There are so many colors out there to choose from, and while you think that yellow text looks fantastic on that orange background...hate to tell you, but no one can read your text anymore.

So what to do? Does your space still not look the way you want it to? Here are some hex code resources for you to check out:

http://www.mundidesign.com/webct/

http://www.visibone.com/colorlab/big.html

Can't pick colors to save your life? Though this doesn't actually give you hex codes (you'll have to take a screenshot and open it in Photoshop, or whatever, to get the hex codes), this is the greatest thing for giving you color palettes that match! It's Behr's paint site! I found out about this when I was thinking about painting my condo and thought it would be perfect for helping to design themes and color palettes: http://www.behr.com/behrx/workbook/ (requires Flash, click Start Color Smart).

For more about the PowerToy Karen mentions in her blog entry, see the section "Adding Special Features with PowerToys" later in this chapter.

The Modules menu lists the modules currently displayed on your space as well as the ones you can add if you'd like (see Figure 7-3). Modules that are currently being used have a Remove link to the right of the module name, and modules that aren't being used have an Add link (meaning that specific module will be added when you click Add). A Delete link appears when you have added a custom module to your space (for example, the Custom List module shown in the figure) that you may want to remove.

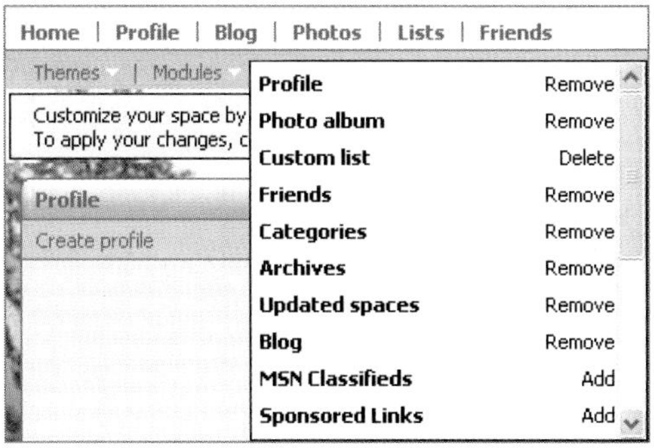

To add a new module to your space, click Add to the right of its name. To remove an existing module,

Figure 7-3: You can easily add or remove modules from your space by clicking the one you want to change.

click Remove to the right of that option. To save your changes to the modules, click the Save button on the right side of the screen beneath the Customize link.

SELECTING A SPACE LAYOUT

The Layout menu displays six layout styles you can choose for your space (see Figure 7-4). The narrow columns are great for lists—music lists, custom lists, the Updated Spaces list, and more. The wider columns are good for your blog or for a large photo album, if that's more your style. Simply click the layout you want to use to select it. Again, click Save to finalize the change.

Figure 7-5 shows a sample space using a two-column layout style. The left column is narrow, and the photo album occupies the wide column, giving plenty of room for photos to be displayed.

If you're the spontaneous type and want to be able to rearrange your space on a whim, you can use the drag-and-drop method of moving modules. (Note, however, that this works only in newer browsers.) In Edit mode, simply click the title bar of a module, and drag it to the new location. A dark outline of the module will move as you drag, and an insert bar will show you where the module will be placed when you release the mouse button. When you have your modules in the places you want them, click Save (at the top of the space) to finalize the changes.

TIP

Figure 7-4: The Layout menu offers six layout styles you can apply to your space.

Figure 7-5: This space uses a two-column layout style and includes the photo album in the wider column.

CREATING A CUSTOM BACKGROUND

If you have a photo you particularly like and you want to make it the background of your space, you can use the Background option to do that. Begin by clicking Save to save the changes you've made to the layout and design of your space. Then click the Background down arrow, and select Choose A Custom Background. The Customize Background tab appears, as shown in Figure 7-6.

To tell MSN Spaces that you want to use a custom photo as the background for your space, click the first option in the Customize Background tab. Then click the Select button to the right of the photo you want to use; scroll down to the bottom of the page, and click Save. This applies the selected photo to your space background.

Adding Special Features with PowerToys

If you're like many space makers, you'll notice that the more you customize your space, the more you *want* to customize your space. You may begin with themes and colors, but this will quickly progress to using your own custom backgrounds, including a few Hypertext Markup Language (HTML) elements (if you're comfortable with the whole coding thing), and experimenting with various layout arrangements.

Figure 7-6: You can add your own image to the background of your page by using the Customize Background tab.

Once you've mastered all the standard cool features MSN Spaces gives you to work with, you might want to scout around on the Web for some extras that can enhance your space. The following sections introduce a few of the special additions MSN Spaces enthusiasts have added successfully to their spaces.

TIP

The following features are undocumented and unsupported by MSN Spaces, so you may want to create a second space to experiment with the features and get comfortable with them before you add them to your main space.

ADDING AUDIO AND VIDEO TO YOUR SPACE

The Windows Media Player PowerToy adds a module to your space that can play audio and video files. This feature can be great fun if you regularly make your own digital video clips or have music segments or voice recordings you want to share with your site visitors. To add the PowerToy, click Edit Your Space, and then position the cursor at the end of the uniform resource locator (URL) in the address bar. Type **&powertoy=musicvideo**, and click Go. After the page loads, click Customize on the right side of your space, and then click the Modules option. In the Modules list, scroll through the list until you see the PowerToy: Windows Media Player option.

Click the Windows Media Player PowerToy module, and the tool is added to your page in Edit mode. Add your video or music clip to the space by entering the URL for where the file is stored in the PowerToy's URL line, as shown in Figure 7-7. (Note: You need to have your own server space in which to store these files; they aren't stored on MSN Spaces.) Click Save beneath the Customize link; then click Preview My Space to see the toy in action.

CAUTION

Although this PowerToy enables you to play video and audio clips on the Web, remember that copyright laws apply. Playing another artist's tunes or showing a clip of someone else's video is illegal without the proper permissions, so stick to using your own custom video or audio recordings with this PowerToy, unless you have the owner's permission.

RADICALLY CUSTOMIZING COLORS

This next MSN Spaces PowerToy (also undocumented, unsupported, and available only in English) isn't for the fainthearted. The Tweak UI PowerToy (UI stands for *user interface*) enables you to change the color and design of all sort of elements on your space: borders, backgrounds, bullets, and more.

Follow the steps described in the previous section for the Windows Media Player PowerToy, but substitute the phrase **&powertoy=tweakomatic** at the end of the URL when you're working in Edit mode. After you click Go and the page reloads, click Customize; then click Modules, scroll down the list, and select PowerToy: Tweak UI. The item is added to your page. Click Save to preserve your changes. Figure 7-8 shows a portion of the customizable settings that are available through this PowerToy.

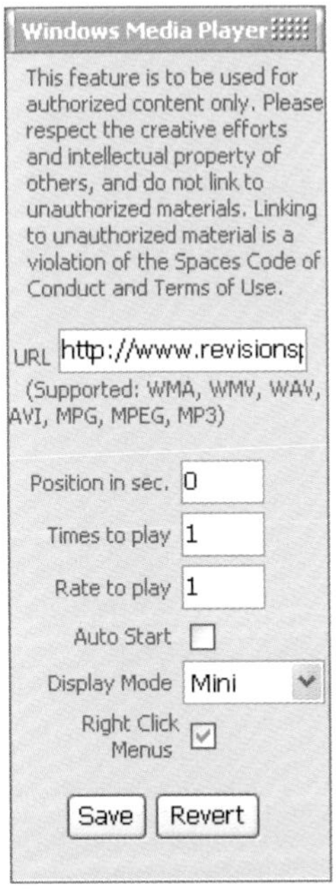

Figure 7-7: Enter the location of the file you want to play on your space.

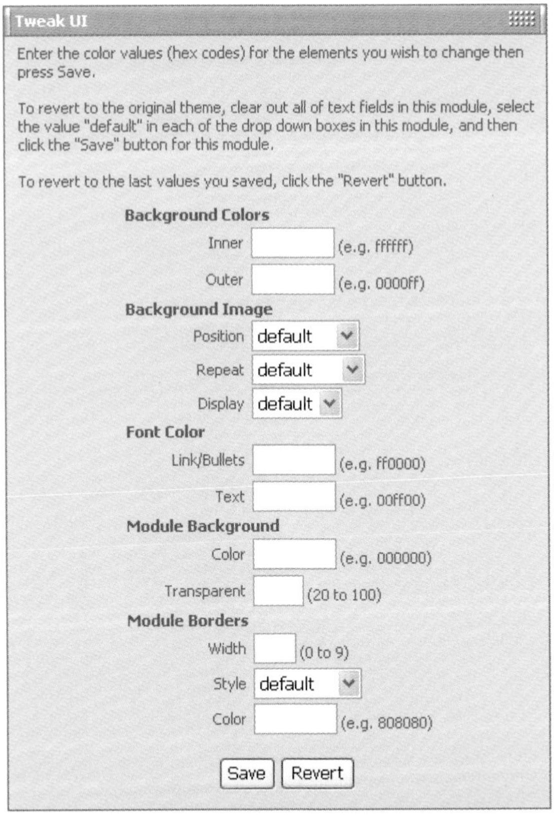

Figure 7-8: The Tweak UI PowerToy is a complex toy that gives you almost unlimited ways to customize the look of your space.

TIP

You need to be familiar with *hex codes* (hexadecimal numeric values assigned to specific colors) in order to work successfully with this customization tool. But they're fun to learn! See the "MSN Backstory: What's in a Theme?" sidebar earlier in this chapter for information about how to get started working with hex values.

PLAYING IN THE HTML SANDBOX

Another PowerToy that appeals to advanced users is the Custom HTML PowerToy, which gives you a "sandbox" for playing with and adding to your space. You could use this Power-Toy, for example, to run a special Web animation you created, to display a page logo, to create an image map, or to do any number of other custom HTML tasks you might be itching to do on your space.

Add this PowerToy the same way you added the others, but insert **&powertoy=sandbox** at the end of the URL before you click Go. Again, add the module to your space, and click Save. A Custom HTML module appears on your space, and you can add HTML code and rename the module to suit your needs (see Figure 7-9). Click Save to keep your changes.

Figure 7-9: The Custom HTML PowerToy enables you to add your own toys in a "sandbox" on your space.

TIP

To keep up on the latest MSN Spaces developments and to find power-user techniques, make sure to save the Space Craft (http://spaces.msn.com/thespace-craft/) in your Favorites list. This space is maintained by the MSN Spaces team, so you're sure to find lots of good info, ideas, suggestions, and solutions here.

A FEW **FUN SANDBOX TOYS**

Here are a few ideas you might want to try with the Custom HTML PowerToy. Note that each of these Web companies provides (usually after you sign in) customized HTML code that you can copy and paste into the Custom HTML module on your space:

- Add a counter to your space so you can keep an eye on how many people have visited it. (Check out http://www.amazingcounters.com to see a variety of available—and free—Web counters.)

- Keep track of how many people are reading your space and where they're coming from by adding a statistics tracker. (Visit http://www.shinystat.com for examples of both displayable and invisible statistic trackers.)

- Add a clock to your space to show visitors what time it is in your corner of the world. (Visit http://www.clocklink.com for some great clocks you can try on your space.)

- **Discovering Updated Spaces through MSN Messenger**

- **Adding Friends to Your Space**

- **Finding New People and Spaces to Visit**

- **Using Spaces Statistics**

Connecting Spaces and Creating Community

CHAPTER 8

MSN Spaces is more than just another Web site for blogging; it's a vibrant and diverse community of people from all over the world connected in some way. MSN Spaces is really all about the people who make it up; people use their spaces as virtual photo books, wedding diaries, personal diaries (blogs), trip journals, and home pages. And the spaces are almost as diverse as the people using them!

MSN Spaces is a vibrant and diverse community of people from all over the world connected in some way.

With MSN Spaces growing at such an incredible rate (at the time of this printing, more than 100,000 new spaces are being created daily), it can sometimes be difficult to find *your place* in this vast expanse. Luckily, not only can you reach out to other people, but you can also easily connect to them, search for stuff, and subscribe to updates so you're never out of touch. This means you'll be able to create your own community using your space by finding and connecting to other people on MSN! Because MSN Messenger and MSN Spaces work together seamlessly, we've included both in this chapter to show you how far your space can reach.

Connecting through MSN Messenger

MSN Messenger is one of the world's most popular software programs with more than 160 million active users. MSN Messenger is used primarily for instant messaging (IM), but it's also popular for having audio and video (A/V) conversations and for sharing files and photos. You can think of MSN Messenger as a gateway to friends and family; when you're interested in chatting (or video-conferencing) with people you care about, all you have to do is fire up MSN Messenger from your Start menu. You'll also be notified when your friends come online, so you can't hide from your parents or old high-school pals anymore.

With the release of MSN Messenger 7 in December 2004, a new feature made it easy to track what your contacts are doing on their spaces. Anytime one of your contacts uploads photos to their space or adds a new blog entry, you'll know within a few minutes (assuming you have access to their space!). This feature is incredibly powerful and is part of the reason spaces are so different from the personal home page trend of the mid-1990s. You don't have to remember to go find your friends' updates—they literally come to you! This feature is called the *gleam*.

> You may be wondering what IM is exactly. IM is really the combination of two complementary technologies: real-time chat and online presence. Typically, real-time chat occurs between two people, but it may also take place with a larger group. *Online presence* is just a fancy phrase for detecting whether someone is online, busy, offline, or away from their desk and for sharing that information with other trusted people.

TIP

> MSN Messenger is different from Windows Messenger, the IM program that is included with Windows XP. The differences run deep and are outside the scope of this book, but you'll need MSN Messenger to use the features described here. If you're running Windows Messenger and don't have MSN Messenger on your PC, you can download and install it from http://messenger.msn.com. MSN Messenger is also available for the Macintosh (it's called Microsoft Messenger) and can be downloaded from http://www.microsoft.com/mac.

NOTE

My Contacts Are "Gleaming"!

Your contact list in MSN Messenger is sort of like your "social dashboard." This is where you can see whether your contacts are online or away, start an IM or A/V conversation with them, and even discover the song to which they're currently listening. The gleam is an indicator that appears next to a contact as soon as their space is updated (see Figure 8-1). When someone's space is first updated, the gleam next to their name in your contact list will actually animate (sort of like a heartbeat) for a few seconds before returning to normal. If you happen to be looking at your MSN Messenger contact list at the time, or you have it open somewhere on your screen, it's pretty hard to miss a gleam when it happens. If you have the window closed or you didn't see the gleam right away, don't worry. The gleam will stick around until you click it (but it won't animate anymore).

Figure 8-1: A gleaming contact in your MSN Messenger contact list, waiting for you to click it

Gleams function just like the "read/unread" status on an e-mail message in most e-mail programs. When you click the gleam to view the contact card (more on that in a bit), the gleam will disappear and stay hidden until the next time that contact updates their space. One of the benefits of the gleam status is that it actually is consistent no matter where you see it. Gleams aren't shown only in MSN Messenger; you can also see them in MSN Hotmail and in parts of MSN Spaces such as blog or photo comments. When you clear the gleam icon in any of those experiences, you won't have to do it again in MSN Messenger; the status "roams" with you! This also means if you have a couple of computers and use MSN Messenger on each of them, you won't have to struggle to remember which updates you've already seen. If you cleared the gleam on one computer, it will be cleared on all of them (assuming you're logging in with the same Microsoft Passport account).

> **NOTE** Gleams are based on some pretty complex privacy rules. People will see a gleam by your name in MSN Messenger (or MSN Hotmail, MSN Spaces, and so on) only if they have access to your space (set in MSN Spaces settings, covered in Chapter 2, "Getting a Space of Your Own"). If for whatever reason their access rights to your space are rescinded, you'll no longer gleam in their contact list when you update your space. You have total control over who is notified.

CONTACT CARDS

Contact cards are like a little peek into someone's space and are most useful when you notice something has changed in his or her space (via the gleam). This is one way to think about it: if a space is someone's room, then the contact card is like looking through the keyhole into the room. You see only a little bit, but you might see enough to entice you to open the door.

Contact cards consist of the most recent updates to a contact's space, and you can open them by clicking the gleam icon (or the MSN Messenger icon) next to a contact's name in MSN Messenger (see Figure 8-2). The information on the top of the card is the most recently updated.

Figure 8-2: A contact card with the most recent changes made to a space

DETAILS ON THE CARD

The following items may occasionally show up on the contact card:

The latest blog entry The title and the first few lines will be shown on the card. If you hover your mouse pointer on the text underneath the title, you'll see a little bit more of the post in a "tooltip."

The last six photos posted to the space in any photo album If you hover your mouse pointer on a photo, you'll see the album name and the name of the photo in a "tooltip."

The most recent additions to a list

An indication that someone's profile was updated

Networking with Friends

MSN Messenger may be one of the most useful programs you have on your computer, and MSN Spaces builds on that potential to give you a place to share what's important to you and connect to other people. Being able to send instant messages, see when your friends come online, or fire up an audio conversation with someone at any time can be incredibly convenient. This functionality has one caveat, though: you usually need to have permission from them before you can communicate with them. And typically to get permission, you need to have their e-mail address to add them as an MSN Messenger contact first. This is usually fine if you happen to share an office with them, but not many people like to publicize their e-mail address these days. This is where "social networking" comes in. With the new social networking features in MSN Messenger and MSN Spaces, you're able to see the friends of your friends and, if they have given you permission, invite them to join MSN Messenger without knowing their e-mail address. This provides a trusted (and fun!) way to find new people to communicate with on MSN Messenger and MSN Spaces.

To view someone's friends in MSN Messenger, right-click the contact in your contact list, and click View Friends. This will open a window with their friends showing (see Figure 8-3). This window, called the Friends Explorer, will let you browse through friends and friends of friends, each time adding the person you're viewing to the breadcrumb trail at the top of the window. Note that this functionality may not be available unless you're using the latest version of MSN Messenger, which is in limited invitation-only beta testing until early 2006. Hopefully by the time you're reading this, if you don't already have it, you'll be able to download it directly from http://messenger.msn.com.

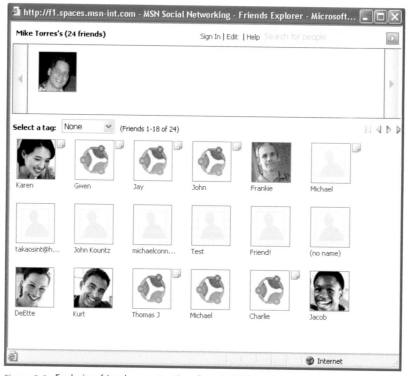

Figure 8-3: Exploring friends one at a time from MSN Messenger

ICONS EVERYWHERE!

When you're viewing someone's friends list in the Friends Explorer (or on their space as part of their friends module), you'll likely see some little icons near their photo (see Figure 8-4).

Figure 8-4: All possible icons that can be associated with a friend. You may never see all these icons at the same time.

This is what each icon means:

Green/red circle   This is their MSN Messenger presence (green is online, and red is offline) and will appear only if you have access to the person's online presence. Clicking it will open a conversation window so you can start chatting with your friend.

Gleam   The gleam you see here is the same one you see in MSN Messenger. It will appear only if this friend has updated their space since the last time you viewed it.

Note   Clicking the note icon will open a "sticky note" with information entered by the owner of the list.

Edit (setup mode only)   Clicking the Edit icon (the pencil) will take you to a page where you can change information about your friend. This icon will appear only if you're in setup mode.

You can also click the down arrow underneath your friend's photo to show the list of actions available for this person. The actions will range from Send IM if the person is already an MSN Messenger contact to Invite To MSN Messenger if they're not. The actions will depend on your relationship to the person you're viewing.

Selecting View Contact Card will not only show the person's contact card but will also clear the gleam icon if it's showing. The details of the contact card depend on whether you have access to the person's space, and just like the card in MSN Messenger, you can flip it over to see the person's contact information.

ADDING FRIENDS TO YOUR FRIENDS LIST

Most people who use the Internet have an address book consisting of people they contact from time to time. These people can range from close friends and family to people they spoke to once at the local pub. Your friends list on MSN Spaces consists of those people from your address book who you'd like to publish as your "friends" for others to see, so it's important to note that this isn't the same list as the private list you see in MSN Messenger (which only you can see). If you want to share your MSN Messenger contact list, you can do that, but you have control over how much to share.

To have a friends list, you'll need to have a space on MSN Spaces (which is probably a given at this point!). But people don't have to have a space, or even visit your space, to see your friends list. Your friends list is accessible from a bunch of different places including MSN Messenger and MSN Hotmail.

You can have up to 500 friends (mutual friends included) in your friends list. Now, we don't know anyone with that many friends...but you may be surprised by how many people pretend to be this popular on the Internet!

Adding friends from your space is pretty easy, especially if you already have an address book in MSN Hotmail or MSN Messenger. If the friends module isn't already showing on your space, you'll need to add it:

 From Edit mode of your space, click the Customize link at the top of the page.

2 Click the Modules drop-down list to view the available modules in MSN Spaces, and select Friends.

3 Click Save to save the layout with your new Friends module.

Before you save the layout, you might want to position the module on the page. To learn more about layout customization, see Chapter 7, "Your Space, Your Way."

4 Now that you have the Friends module on the page, you'll need to open the setup page to start adding friends. To do this, click the Edit link on the newly added Friends module.

The setup page should open in a pop-up window.

5 To add a new friend, click the Add A Friend link at the top of the window.

On the next page (see Figure 8-5), you'll see four ways to add new friends to your friends list. You can add them via an e-mail address, via a space URL, from your MSN Messenger contact list, or from your MSN address book.

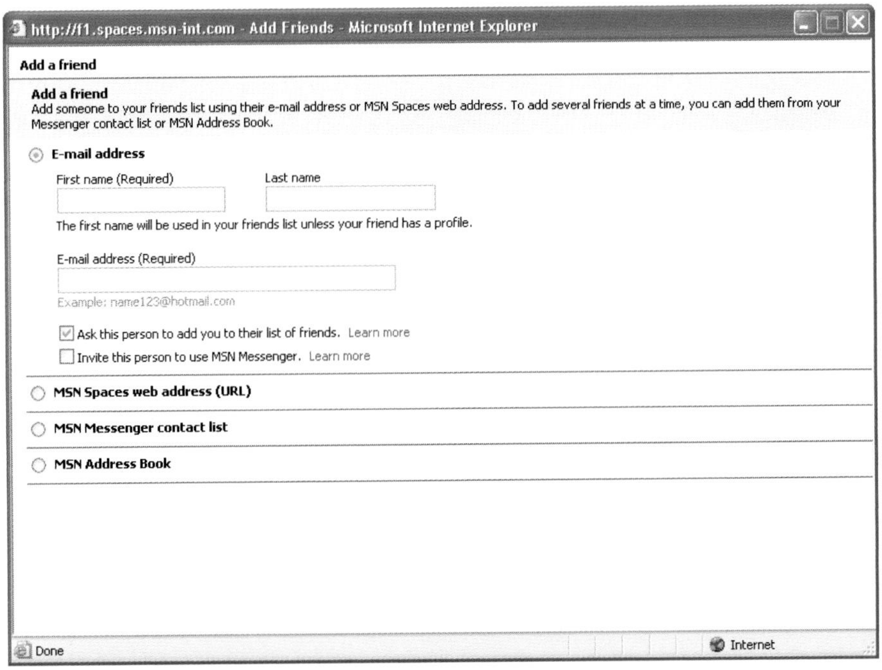

Figure 8-5: Adding a friend in one of four different ways

WHAT IS A MUTUAL FRIEND?

A *mutual friend* is someone who appears on your friends list and also has you on their friends list. This is sometimes referred to as a *reciprocal*, or two-way, relationship. You can tell the difference between friends and mutual friends by looking closely at how they appear in the friends list.

Here is a quick rundown:

- If someone is a mutual friend, they will be shown with either their profile photo or a silhouette icon. The silhouette icon is used if they don't have a profile photo or if the permission level on their profile photo isn't set so that everyone can access it.

- If someone isn't a mutual friend, you'll see an MSN Spaces logo.

Here is how it actually works behind the scenes: Mike adds Julie to his friends list. If Julie also has Mike in her friends list, Mike and Julie are mutual friends. This means someone viewing Mike's friends list will immediately be able to tell that Julie also knows Mike. In other words, Julie has Mike as a friend as well.

A similar process takes place when you remove a friend from your friends list. For example, if Mike were to remove Julie from his friends list, Mike would be demoted from a mutual friend in Julie's list, and it would appear as if they're not connected at all.

Here is a little more information on each approach:

E-mail address   You should use this option if you have your friend's e-mail address and you'd like to make them a friend. The e-mail address doesn't have to be a Microsoft Passport address; you can add any e-mail address to your friends list and choose to have an e-mail sent to your friend. Your friend will need to create a Microsoft Passport before they can create a profile on MSN Profile or a friends list of their own, however. Until they do that, they will never show up as a mutual friend in your list. If you'd like an e-mail sent to your friend, check the box indicating that an invitation should be sent. If you'd like to make your friend an MSN Messenger contact, check that box as well.

> For e-mail addresses and space URLs, these invitations will be sent only if their communications preferences allow them to be! The First Name field is required along with the e-mail address or space URL; the First Name setting is what will be used in your friends list until your friend creates a profile on MSN Profile. If they already have a profile, the name they have chosen will be used in your list instead, and the name you just entered will be ignored.

NOTE

Space URL   You should use this option if you don't have your friend's e-mail address and have only their URL. Just like with e-mail, if you'd like an e-mail sent to your friend, check the box indicating that an invitation should be sent. If you'd like to make your friend an MSN Messenger contact, check that box as well.

MSN Messenger contact list and MSN address book   You should use this option to add more than one friend at once. And again, just like previously, if you'd like an e-mail sent to your friends, check the box indicating that an invitation should be sent. (These invitations will be sent only if their communications preferences allow them to be.) Also, the first name for the contact in your address book is how they will be displayed in your friends list until your friend creates a profile on MSN Profile. If they already have a profile, the name they have chosen will be used in your list instead, and the name you just entered will be ignored. In case your friend doesn't have a first name in your address book, "no name" will be used, and you'll have to manually edit your friend's name later.

When you're finished adding friends, you'll see a confirmation page. The confirmation page is a little different depending on whether you're adding multiple friends or adding just one. A helpful legend on this page gives you a little more information on the types of icons that may appear next to your friends in your friends list.

TAGGING YOUR FRIENDS AND ADDING NOTES

Every relationship you have with someone is different from the next. The reasons you're friends with people can vary a great deal, and the features that are special about each of your friends can vary just as much. You may have a friend who is a great teacher and another who has amazing photography skills. Similarly, you may have friends from work, from school, from your childhood...or your friends may really be family members or your spouse. How do you make this clear to other people looking at your friends list? You can add tags or notes to your friends for others to see wherever your friends list appears, whether it's in your friends module in MSN Spaces or the Friends Explorer in MSN Messenger. A tag is a phrase you would associate with a friend (that is, "loyal"), while a note is a short commentary.

To add tags and notes, you need to first edit a friend:

① From Edit mode of your space, click Edit on the friends list that is showing on your space. If your friends list isn't showing, see the earlier "Adding Friends to Your Friends List" section.

② When the Friends window opens, click the Edit icon (the pencil) of the person to whom you'd like to apply the tags or notes.

The Edit page will open (see Figure 8-6). From this page, you'll be able to add tags and notes and choose whether your friend should appear near the top or the bottom of your friends list.

TIP When you're viewing someone else's friends, it's easy to see which tags they have applied to people. Just open the note next to their photo (the little note icon). You can also filter on a specific tag to see all the friends who have that tag.

TAG—YOU'RE IT!

Adding tags to your friends is super easy. Let's take a look how to add a "basketball" tag to Andy from the Edit page. First, add the word *basketball* into the Tag area, and click Add. This will apply the word *basketball* to Andy.

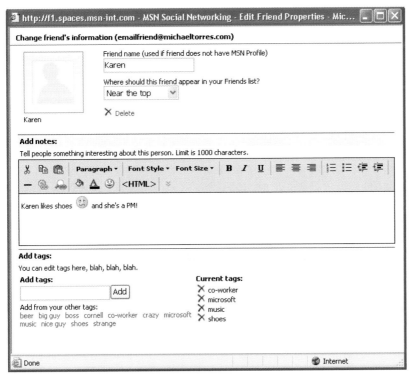

Figure 8-6: The Edit page gives you flexibility in how you'd like your friends to be shown.

Once you've applied tags to your friends, you'll be able to reuse those tags for other friends easily. Underneath the tag area, you'll see your previous tags prepopulated. When one of the tags is clicked, it will fill the box above it and will be applied to your friend as soon as you click Add.

To remove a tag, just click the Delete icon next to the tag in the Current Tags list.

NOTE

You can add 15 tags to a friend, and each tag has a maximum length of 20 characters (including any spaces).

NOTES—DESCRIBING YOUR FRIENDSHIPS

Notes are a fun way to associate text with your friends. You can type anything you want, and other people viewing your friends list will be able to read what you write by clicking the note icon next to your friend's profile photo in your friends list (see Figure 8-7 for an example within MSN Spaces). You can do this when you're viewing someone's friends through MSN Messenger, too.

Figure 8-7: Viewing notes on people can be insightful; you never know what people are going to say!

You can use notes to describe your friend, talk about how you met or why you two are friends, or make a little fun of them. Unlike tags, notes can contain *rich text*, which is just a fancy way of saying you can use bold, italics, and smiley faces to your heart's content. You can even insert raw Hypertext Markup Language (HTML) if you're so inclined (but just like in blog entries, anything that could be malicious is stripped out before it makes it into the MSN Spaces system). To add notes to a contact, use the input form on the friend's Edit page.

NOTE Notes are limited to 1,024 characters (including spaces), so choose your words wisely.

PUTTING YOUR FRIENDS IN THEIR PLACE

When you're adding notes and tags to your friends, you can also choose where you'd like your friends to appear in your friends list—near the top, near the bottom, or "doesn't matter." These settings aren't absolute; if you have 15 friends and would like them to appear "near the top," you won't know exactly where they will appear in those first 15 positions. But this does give you some basic sorting ability in case you want to make sure a family member isn't relegated to the fifth page!

However, you can use a little trick to make sure one of your friends appears exactly where you'd like them to appear in your list. You do this simply by adding a special tag to your friend to indicate their exact sort position. Give one of these a try:

- Add "Sort:1" as a tag (no spaces, no quotes) to your best friend. When you click Done on the Edit page and return to the main page, your best friend should appear first in your list!

- Add "Sort:1000" as a tag to the person on your list you rarely talk to anymore. When you click Done on the Edit page and return to the main page, this person should appear in the last position on the list.

These tags don't show up as viewable tags applied to your friends; the system automatically hides them. If you'd like to change the sort position of one of your friends, all you have to do is add the tag again with the new value. For example, if the person you placed at the end of the list gets you a really great gift for your birthday, you can promote them to the second position just by adding "Sort:2" as a tag.

Note that if you mistakenly tag two friends with the same position (say, "Sort:1"), the system will randomly make a determination as to whom should appear first, but their relative position in the list will be maintained. In other words, your friends would randomly appear as first and second if they were both tagged with "Sort:1."

SETTING THE FRIEND NAME

The Friend Name field on the Edit page is used in your friends list only if your friend doesn't have a profile on MSN Profile. Once your friend gets a profile, the name that appears in your friends list will be the name they have chosen to go by in their profile (their display name). In case MSN Spaces doesn't have a name for this friend, you may see "no name" in this textbox.

DELETING FRIENDS

Tired of someone? Delete them! To delete someone from your friends list, all you have to do is click the Delete link from your friend's Edit page. They will immediately be removed from your list, and if you were mutual friends, you'll no longer be a mutual friend in their list.

Searching for People and Spaces

One of the most popular ways to find information on the Internet is to use a search engine. Finding information about people in the MSN Spaces community is no different. The first step most people take when they want to find out who the U.S. president was in 1948, for example, is to fire up a search engine, so it's only natural you'd do the same when you want to find people interested in knitting, for example, on MSN Spaces.

To search MSN Spaces, all you have to do is visit http://spaces.msn.com. On this page, you'll find a search box (the blue one, not the green one!) to start your search (see Figure 8-8).

RESULTS: MORE THAN JUST A LINK

If you've ever used a traditional search engine such as Google, Yahoo, or MSN Search (and who hasn't?), you're probably used to the results looking like a long list of blue hyperlinks with a little bit of description text below them. The links, while useful when searching for specific text on a page, aren't that useful if you're searching for a date—or for your prom date from the 1980s. Sometimes pictures tell a thousand words. And even when they don't, they're still typically more fun to look at than a list of links.

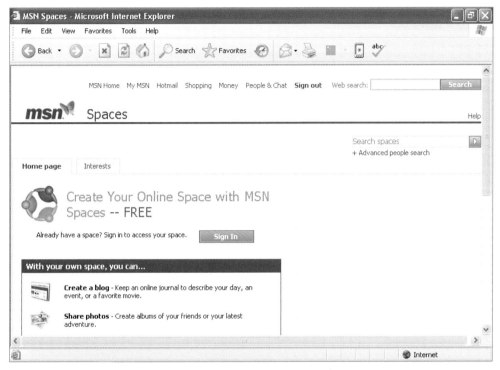

Figure 8-8: The MSN Spaces home page where you'll begin your search

MSN Spaces Search incorporates profile photos into the search results to give you more information about the person. And just like the friends list, the information isn't limited to just the photo! You can see this person's name and whether they're online

or they've updated their space (if you have access to this information). You can also invite them to join MSN Messenger, visit their profile or their space, and invite them to become a friend, amongst other things. You can open the actions that are listed, just like the friends list, by clicking the little arrow beneath the person's photo.

Maya Voskoboynikov, a program manager for MSN Spaces, describes the search results this way: "When you want to find people online—whether it's an old friend you're trying to locate or just someone in your town who shares your love of reading— you want to get back *people* in your results, not text links." (You can find Maya at http://spaces.msn.com/members/mayav.)

NOTE

Unless you're using Internet Explorer 6 (and greater) or Mozilla Firefox 1.0 (and greater), you may not see the actions appear as an option underneath a person's photo. Unfortunately, the actions aren't supported in every browser on the market.

The search results also give you the ability to narrow your search further by clicking the headers in the results. For example, if you're interested only in blog entries, you can click the Blog Entries heading or the View More Results link to the right of it to see a page full of blog entries. Ditto for spaces or people (profile-only) results (see Figure 8-9).

Figure 8-9: The search results page. From here you can drill down further into blog entries, spaces, or people (profile-only).

Search results in MSN Spaces also have corresponding RSS feeds provided by MSN Search. This means you can subscribe to a feed in your favorite reader and watch as the results change over time. See Appendix A, "RSS Q&A: Interview with an RSS Aficionado," for an overview of RSS.

TIP

BROWSING BY INTEREST

When you set up your profile, chances are you chose interests to associate with it. If your profile is public, this means people can actually search for people with similar interests and stumble upon *you*! You also have another way to find people by interest—the MSN Spaces Interests page (see Figure 8-10). This page shows you all

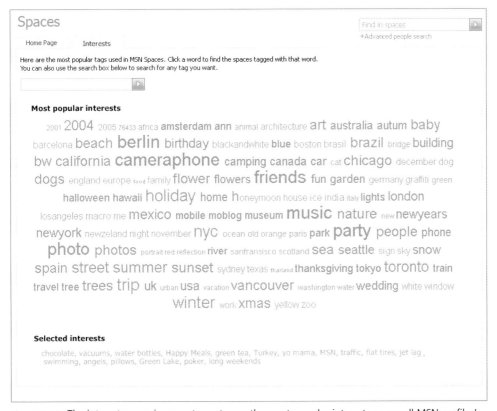

Figure 8-10: The interests page is a great way to see the most popular interests across all MSN profiles!

the most popular interests across MSN Spaces, with more popular interests appearing larger than less popular interests. At the bottom of the page, you'll find selected (or sponsored) interests, which will be updated from time to time by the MSN Spaces staff.

You can find this page by clicking Interests on the MSN Spaces home page at http://spaces.msn.com.

You can also do an interest-only search from this page. (Note that this is also available with the Advanced People Search feature, which we'll discuss next.) Just type any interest into the search box on this page to find people matching that interest!

ADVANCED PEOPLE SEARCH

Searching for people by keyword isn't always the most productive use of your time, especially when you know exactly who you're looking for or you have a general idea in your head of the *kind* of person you'd like to find. A textbox doesn't make it easy to find someone named Robert Scoble living in Seattle, Washington, without a little bit of elbow grease. Instead of trying to shoehorn the description of a person into a textbox, the Advanced People Search feature lets you search for specific attributes.

You can search by these specifics:

- First name
- Last name
- Gender
- Age range
- Location
- Occupation
- Interests
- Interested in meeting

You don't have to fill in every field for an advanced people search; they're all optional. For example, you can search for women, age 25–29, in a specific ZIP code. Or you could search for all people with your last name or everyone from your hometown who shares your interest in skydiving.

To use the Advanced People Search feature, just click the Advanced People Search link underneath the Search box on the MSN Spaces home page.

UPDATED SPACES PAGE

Browsing random spaces can kill time even faster than 34 games of Freecell. To see the 100 most recently updated spaces, just browse to http://spaces.msn.com/ morespaces.aspx, or click the More link on the home page. Be careful, though—it's easy to get lost in there!

Eric Swanson, an independent developer, was frustrated one day with the Updated Spaces page and decided to create his own. His site has become popular with MSN Spaces users. It goes beyond the standard Updated Spaces page and gives you more information about the spaces on the list, such as profile photo, number of posts, last entry title, and even search functionality.

To check out Eric's revised Updated Spaces page, go to http://www.andnbsp .com/. His space is available at http://spaces.msn.com/members/eswanson.

For other developers, an XML document lists the most recently updated spaces in reverse order. The page is available at http://spaces.msn.com/ changes.aspx but isn't "officially supported" by Microsoft. The format follows the changes.xml standard documented at http://newhome.weblogs.com/ changesXml.

TIP

Stats: Find Out Who Is Visiting Your Space

One of the best ways to kill time on a Sunday afternoon is to see how people are finding your space. Sometimes it's surprising to discover how people end up in your world; it may be via search engines or from a link on a friend's space. It may be because they've subscribed to your space in an RSS reader. However they've found you, it's always fun to see where they are coming from.

To open your statistics, follow these steps:

1. From Edit mode of your space, click Settings near the top of the page.

2. Once in Settings, click Statistics.

From this page (see Figure 8-11), you'll be able to see a bunch of numbers:

Total page views   This is the total number of times any page on your space has been viewed since you started it.

Page views today   This is the total number of page views your space has received in the last 24 hours.

Page views this week   This is the total number of page views your space has received since Sunday at 12 A.M.

Page views within the last hour   This is the number of page views your space has received in the past hour.

The table below the statistics is the *referrer log*. It's a reverse chronological list of "hits" to your space. You can see the date/time the hit occurred, the page title (the page viewed), and the referring address. The referring address (sometimes also just called a *referrer*) is probably the most interesting item in the table. It indicates how people found your space. For example, if someone clicked a link on someone else's space to end up on your space, that person's space would be listed as the referrer.

These are the other items you might see in your referrer log:

Search engines   If you look closely in the URL of the search engine, you'll be able to find the search query used to find your space. For example, Google searches show up like this: http://www.google.com/search?hl=en&q=windows+vista. In the

URL, you can see the words *windows vista* embedded. This indicates that someone searched for *windows vista* and found your space!

Other people's spaces   This will include links from their friends list and links from their blog, lists, or comments. If someone found your space by clicking a link in someone else's space, you'll see that!

Other Web pages or blogs   If someone linked to your space from their blog or another Web page (such as a news article or a message board post), that link will show up in your referrer log.

> If someone uses their bookmarks or Favorites list to visit your space, or if they typed in your URL directly, you won't be able to tell this. The referrer is listed only if a link is clicked from another source.

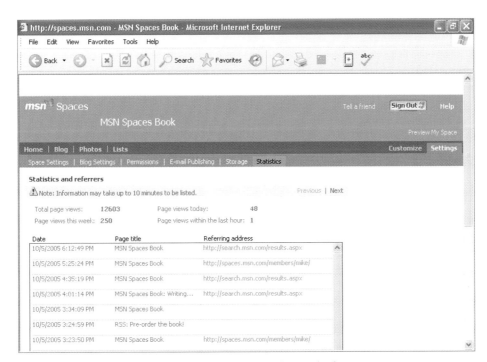

Figure 8-11: From your statistics page you can see page views and referrers.

Extending Your Spaces Experience

CHAPTER 9

By now you've learned a huge amount about MSN Spaces—you know how to sign up for a Microsoft Passport, create your space, post blog entries, add photos, create lists, invite friends, customize your space, and share your work with the world. Maybe the best feature of using MSN Spaces to connect with others and share your creative energy is that not a bit of your work goes to waste! Because MSN Spaces is part of a larger MSN communications family, you can use the other MSN programs to help you bring content and visitors to your space seamlessly. That's what this chapter shows you how to do.

Using MSN Messenger: The Hub of the (Communications) World

Maybe the best feature of using MSN Spaces to connect with others and share your creative energy is that not a bit of your work goes to waste!

MSN Messenger is a free instant messaging program that enables you to communicate online in real time with friends, family, and co-workers by typing quick messages or sending voice or video messages. MSN Messenger organizes your online contacts and shows you their status—*who is online right now?*—and gives you multiple ways of connecting with the people you want to communicate with in an easy-to-use window (see Figure 9-1). The blue icons show contacts who are currently online, the red icons identify your contacts who are offline, and the gold icons show which of your contacts are available by cell phone.

To connect with one of your online contacts, simply double-click the person's contact name, and a message window opens (see Figure 9-2). You can then type a quick note and click Send (or press Enter); your message pops up on the other person's desktop immediately.

From the MSN Messenger window, you can reach all sorts of information (see Figure 9-3). The title bar shows you how many messages you have waiting for you in your MSN Hotmail account. It also gives you a link to your space on MSN Spaces so you can move right to your space without opening your Web browser and entering the address. Additionally, you can click the MSN Today link on the right if you want to see what's happening in the world.

NOTE In addition to giving you instant ways to connect with others online, MSN Messenger brings together in one place many different kinds of information—from groups to stocks to entertainment news to tech updates.

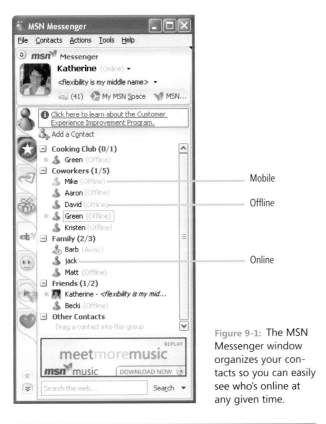

Mobile

Offline

Online

Figure 9-1: The MSN Messenger window organizes your contacts so you can easily see who's online at any given time.

Figure 9-2: When you double-click an online contact, a message window opens so you can start the conversation.

MSN Hotmail

MSN Today

MSN Spaces

Figure 9-3: You can get to MSN Hotmail, MSN Spaces, and MSN Today all from within MSN Messenger.

GETTING STARTED WITH MSN MESSENGER

If you have your own space, you already have a Microsoft Passport. That means all you have to do to use MSN Messenger is go to the Web site and download the software. Navigate to http://messenger.msn.com/, and click the Download Now! button (see Figure 9-4). Follow the on-screen prompts to download and install MSN Messenger. In just a few minutes, you'll be up and running with MSN Messenger.

After you've installed and started MSN Messenger following the on-screen instructions, the program displays a welcome screen and invites you to add contacts to your MSN Messenger window (see Figure 9-5). You can create a contact by entering the other person's e-mail address or cell phone number. MSN Messenger then helps you compose an e-mail message to that person inviting them to download and use MSN Messenger so that the two of you can communicate in real-time online (see Figure 9-6).

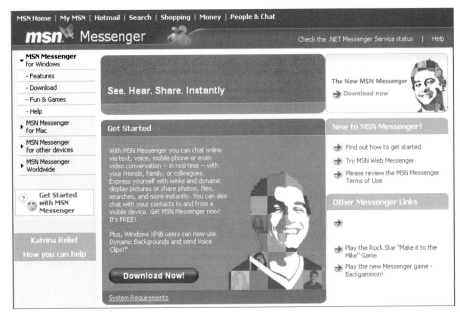

Figure 9-4: It takes just a few minutes to download and install MSN Messenger—and it's free!

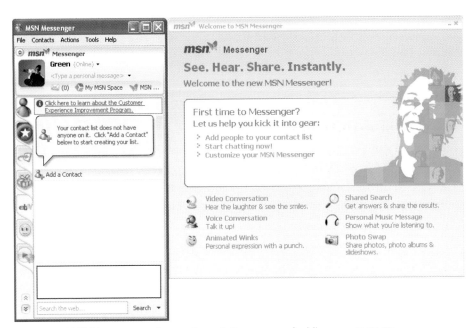

Figure 9-5: MSN Messenger walks you through the process of adding new contacts.

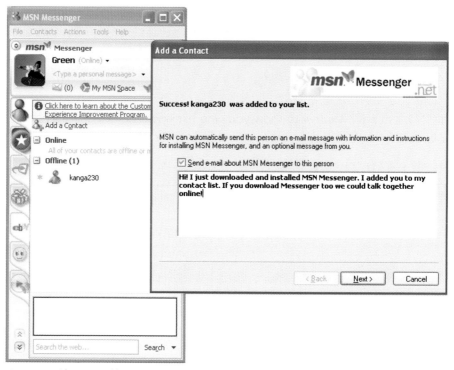

Figure 9-6: After you add a contact, you can send a customizable e-mail message with more information about MSN Messenger.

MSN MESSENGER BENEFITS FOR MSN SPACES USERS

So, you can see that MSN Messenger is a fun way to stay in touch with people you know and work with—but what does that have to do with MSN Spaces? Using MSN Messenger and MSN Spaces together has a number of benefits—in fact, they complement each other well. Here's a rundown of the ways these two programs together help you extend your MSN Spaces experience:

Announce your updates   Your "gleam" shows the people in your Contacts list that something new is on your space. (For a more information, see Chapter 8, "Connecting Spaces and Creating Community.")

Stay in touch   MSN Messenger helps you stay in instant touch with people on your Contacts list and helps them see when you've updated your space.

Update easily   You can post directly to your space by choosing an option from your MSN Messenger menu.

See who you need to read   A "gleam" appears to the left of a contact name in the MSN Messenger window to show you who has updated their space since your last visit. (Again, check this feature out in Chapter 8.)

Show off your space   By clicking your "gleam," your contacts can display your contact card, complete with your profile picture, latest space information, and thumbnails of your most recently posted photos.

Have you heard of MSN Web Messenger? It's the totally Web-based cousin of MSN Messenger that enables you to enjoy instant messaging features on the Web without downloading the MSN Messenger software to your computer. Find out more about it by going to http://webmessenger.msn.com.

TIP

POSTING TO YOUR SPACE FROM MSN MESSENGER

Suppose that you've just returned to your office after a nice lunch break with a co-worker. You decide to take a minute and add a note on your space about the great restaurant you found. To post directly to your space without leaving MSN Messenger, follow these steps:

1. In MSN Messenger, click the down arrow to the right of your username. A submenu appears, as shown in Figure 9-7.

2. Click Add To My Personal Space. MSN Spaces opens directly to the Edit Blog Entry page, where you can type your post, click Publish Entry, and get back to work (see Figure 9-8).

Figure 9-7: You can go right to your space to create a blog entry from MSN Messenger.

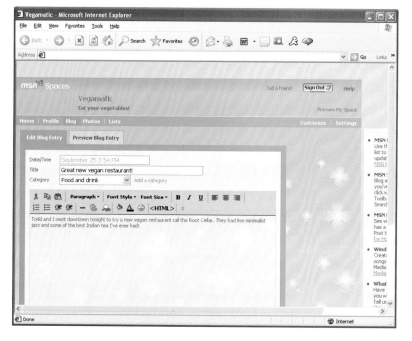

Figure 9-8: Compose your post, and click Publish Entry to update your space.

YOU'VE GOT THE "GLEAM"

The MSN Messenger "gleam" is a little bit of genius packed inside a program. With a simple little sparkle, you can let all the contacts in your list know that your space has been updated since the last time they visited. What's more, when a contact clicks your gleam, your contact card appears, showing your profile picture, the first line of your most recent post, and any photos you've uploaded recently. It's a great little bit of publicity for your space, all coming from a little gold gleam (see Figure 9-9).

> Chapter 8, "Connecting Spaces and Creating Community," covers this in much more detail, but we have included it here because it's a great link between the MSN Messenger and MSN Spaces experiences.
>
> NOTE

Figure 9-9: Clicking the gleam opens the contact card so people can preview changes on your space.

DOING THE MATH AND GETTING YOUR SPACE NOTICED

If you're new to the world of online publishing, you may not have given too much thought yet to how you'll get your space noticed. But as you get comfortable using MSN Spaces and begin to enjoy checking out the statistics and watching the number of hits you get on your space, you'll see that getting noticed is fun. You have something to say to the world—and the world is listening!

Here are some numbers you may be interested in: currently MSN Hotmail has an estimated 200 million active users, and MSN Messenger has more than 150 million active users. And MSN Spaces is climbing fast—by the time you read this, it will probably have close to 50 million active users!

When you consider that this is just a small part of the total number of Web users, you get the sense that an enormous potential audience could just stumble across your space one day! A single post on a relevant topic could get you picked up by a search engine and catapulted to the Web spotlight for an hour, for a day, or—who knows?— for an extended period of time. Just to put these numbers in context, one MSN Spaces user posted a blog entry about a hot topic that was showing up in search engines all over the world. His space got a small mention (and a link) on the MSN.com home page, and that day he had more than 200,000 visitors to his space! If you're looking for a little attention for your space, that's like hitting the jackpot!

MSN Hotmail and MSN Spaces: Making Connections via Contacts

In the future it's likely that MSN Spaces and MSN Hotmail will be tighter companions than they are right now. (A revolutionary new release of MSN Hotmail is currently in the works but won't be available publicly for awhile.) For now, however, a number of shared features can make your MSN Spaces experience more integrated with your everyday work.

As you learned earlier in the chapter, you can see how many MSN Hotmail messages are waiting for you simply by looking at the top of the MSN Messenger window (gosh, we have 41 messages waiting?); you can move directly to Hotmail by clicking the mail icon. In the top-left side of the MSN Hotmail window, you can see that the program registers your MSN Messenger online status (see Figure 9-10).

Although MSN Spaces isn't visible in the simple Inbox area of MSN Hotmail, you'll find MSN Spaces connections on the Contacts tab. Click Contacts to display your Contacts list. As shown in Figure 9-11, you can see which of your contacts are currently online. When you click the contact card icon, a version of the card opens, showing you the person's space name, recently added text, and thumbnails of any uploaded photos (see Figure 9-12). You can click the link to move directly to their space or click the mail icon to compose an MSN Hotmail message to them.

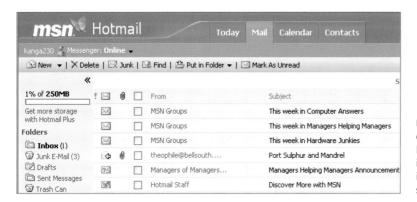

Figure 9-10: Move directly into MSN Hotmail by clicking the mail icon in the MSN Messenger window.

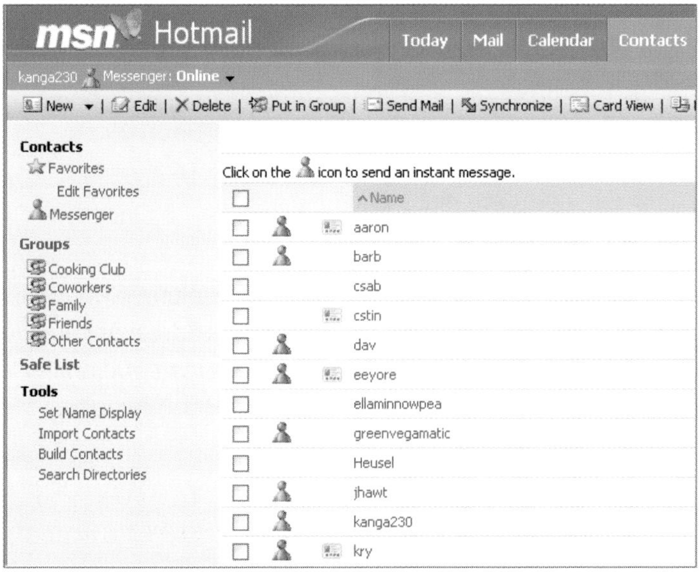

Figure 9-11: The MSN Hotmail Contacts list shows you the online status of your contacts and gives you a way to move directly to their spaces.

Figure 9-12: The contact card enables you to see a bit of the recent space update and click to find out more.

MSN Spaces, MSN Hotmail, and MSN Messenger—Three Tools in One

We'll round out this chapter with a brief example of a scenario in which you can use all three communications programs together in a way that enables you to share your ideas quickly and easily with those who will be most interested in them:

Start with MSN Messenger Suppose that you've just logged on in the morning and your MSN Messenger window opens automatically. The MSN Today window shows a link that catches your eye—a healthy new recipe for something you've been wanting to try. You click the link to find out more.

Stop over at MSN.com You're taken to the Web site listing the article you wanted to read. The recipe is really good, and you want to share it with your cooking group. You highlight the recipe and press Ctrl+C to copy it. Then you scroll down to the bottom of the page, where you see a Hotmail link (see Figure 9-13). You click the link to open MSN Hotmail.

Move on to Hotmail In the MSN Hotmail window, you click New to compose a new message and press Ctrl+V to paste the recipe into it. You then click To and select your Cooking Group contact, which includes the e-mail address of your space about vegetarian cooking, which you set up to receive e-mail publishing from this MSN Hotmail account (see Figure 9-14). (See Chapter 2, "Getting a Space of Your Own," for more information about setting up your space for e-mail publishing.) This means you can e-mail the information once—to others in your group and to your space—instead of duplicating your effort by sending an e-mail and posting to your space separately.

Check out your space   Depending on how you set up your space to receive e-mail posts—to save them as drafts or to publish them directly to your space—you may need to go to your space to finalize the post. (Until you really get the hang of mobile publishing, saving the posts as drafts is the best way to go.) Go to your space by clicking the Messenger link on the left side of the MSN Hotmail toolbar, and then click My MSN Space to view your space. The e-mail post will be waiting on you (see Figure 9-15)!

> Remember to ask for permission to use others' work and give proper credit for anything you publish on your space that isn't yours. To stay on the right side of the copyright issue, you might simply want to write a little overview of what you found and then link to the original work on the owner's site. If you do reproduce part of an author's work on your site (after getting his or her permission), be sure to link to the original and give the author credit.
>
> CAUTION

Source: http://wine.msn.com/?article.aspx?aid=68&GT1=6983

Figure 9-13: Scroll down to find the Hotmail link at the bottom of the page.

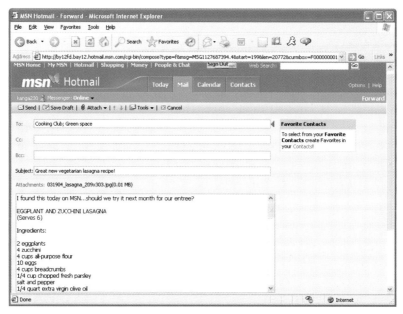

Figure 9-14: You can e-mail a post to your space if you have set up e-mail publishing in MSN Spaces.

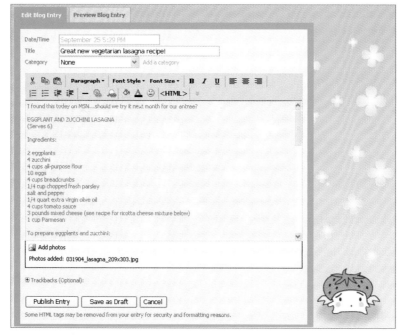

Figure 9-15: The e-mail post, which started as an interesting link you found through MSN Messenger, traveled through MSN Hotmail and is now a part of your space on MSN Spaces.

A QUIET SPACE: JUST FRIENDS AND FAMILY, PLEASE

Not everybody wants to have thousands of fans clamoring for the latest update on their space. Some people just want a simple space they can update to show their latest pictures to their closest friends and family. Uncle Henry lives in Bolivia, and you want to show him the photos of the strawberry crop this year. Cousin Sean in Chicago missed your sister's wedding, and you've posted the photos (and a video clip of the cake-cutting ceremony) so he can feel like part of the event.

MSN Messenger helps you stay in touch with your family and provides the same gleam and contact card to all those on your list. If you have your MSN Spaces permission set to Private or to Messenger only, you can protect your space so you don't get the masses knocking at your proverbial cyberdoor. Your MSN Messenger window will also continue to display gleams for other spaces you may be interested in reading (and for those who have permission to visit your space), and MSN Hotmail lists the online/offline status for all those on your list, no matter how your permissions are set for your space. So, see? You can have the best of both: a quick relaxing family space *and* a window to the world.

RSS Q&A: Interview with an RSS Aficionado

APPENDIX A

RSS is nothing short of a revolution in Web publishing. In just a few short years, RSS, which stands for Really Simple Syndication, has grown from a nascent technology to the primary means of syndication on the Web. Syndication means that you can automatically have the content from your space delivered to the readers who want to receive it. It's simple, it's fast, and it's the wave of the future. Read on for some basics about RSS and an interview with a true RSS enthusiast (and coauthor of this book), Mike Torres.

It's simple, it's fast, and it's the wave of the future.

What Do You Need to Read an RSS Feed?

If you're new to RSS, you may be drawing a blank about this relatively new technology. When you subscribe to a Web site in order to receive updates in the form of an RSS feed, the data (both text and images) from that site is delivered directly to you (as opposed to you having to go to the site to read the information). You read the RSS feed using a utility known as an *RSS reader*. You can download several free RSS readers from the Web; popular RSS readers include SharpReader, Feedreader, NewsGator, and RSS Bandit. Additionally, you can use a Web-based RSS reader such as Start.com to view all your RSS content online.

Publishing an RSS Feed

Every space on MSN Spaces publishes an RSS feed by default if the space's permissions are set to Public, meaning there's no restriction on who can view the space. If the space is set to Private, the RSS feed can't be produced and is temporarily disabled until the permissions are set to Public. To turn on RSS syndication for your space, follow these steps:

1. Click Edit Your Page to display your space in Edit mode.

2. Click Settings near the top of the page.

③ Click Space Settings, and scroll down to Syndicate. Click the checkbox to turn on the RSS feature. (If the option is disabled, check your space permissions, and make sure they are set to Public.)

④ Click Save to save the change to your space.

Now people will be able to subscribe to your RSS feed by clicking Syndicate Using RSS at the top of your space.

RSS Q&A Interview with Mike Torres

Mike Torres is a lead program manager for MSN Spaces, the coauthor of this book, and a true RSS expert and enthusiast. To help round out the discussion of RSS, Mike shares his interests and ideas about RSS with us:

Q: What is RSS, and why should MSN Spaces users care about it?

A: RSS stands for Really Simple Syndication (or Rich Site Summary, depending on who you ask). It's a method of describing Web site content in a way that other Web sites and desktop programs (called *news readers* or *aggregators*) can retrieve the content and do snazzy things with it, such as letting users read blog posts or search through news articles. Best of all, these programs will bug you only when new stuff has been added to your favorite sites. Because of this, it's especially useful for blogs and news sites that contain collections of individual items updated frequently.

RSS plays a key role in MSN Spaces. Because every public space has the ability to publish a feed for others to subscribe to, people can use their favorite reader to be notified of updates. RSS from MSN Spaces makes it incredibly easy to not only see when spaces have been updated but also to read blog posts or preview photo albums from within a reader.

Every MSN Space publishes an RSS feed by default if the permissions on the space are set to Public. If the space is set to Private, the RSS feed can't be produced and is temporarily disabled until the permissions are set to Public. You can check to see whether an RSS is being produced for your space by looking in Space Settings.

For more information about RSS, including a little history, read the entry on Wikipedia at http://en.wikipedia.org/wiki/RSS_(protocol).

Q: How does RSS make your life better? Do you receive an enormous number of RSS feeds daily?

A: I'm truly an information junkie and love to know about events immediately as they happen. A few years ago (in my pre-RSS days), I would visit about 20 to 30 Web sites every day just to discover they hadn't changed at all since the day before. After doing this for a while, you start to wonder why there isn't a better way to stay up-to-date on topic in which you're interested. Turns out there was...I just didn't know about it.

Today, I am able to track more than 325 different feeds multiple times per day. Since I have to read only the content that has changed since the last time I read the feed, I can scan all 325+ feeds in less than 45 minutes per day and even have time left to comment on some of the items. To some people, 45 minutes a day may sound like a lot—but in an industry like ours where information is a valuable currency, to be able to track 325+ different information sources daily in less than 45 minutes is really pretty remarkable.

One of the best uses of RSS for me is the ability to subscribe to search results from blog search engines (PubSub, Technorati, Feedster, IceRocket) as well as some of the major search engines such as MSN and Yahoo. For example, I subscribe to the key-word search *MSN Spaces sucks* so I know immediately when someone is having a problem with MSN Spaces! The team has been able to quickly get a read on the "connected conversations" out there when it comes to MSN Spaces, and we have surprised a lot of people by dropping in to let them know we care!

Q: Which RSS reader do you use? Is there a reason you use that one over others?

A: I use Bloglines at http://www.bloglines.com. The following is a blog entry from December 10th, 2004, outlining some of the reasons why I use it, which still hold true a year later:

WHY I DIG BLOGLINES

Source: http://spaces.msn.com/members/mike/Blog/cns!1pG4qKNdtRA5Nl-UhvZl_1rQ!570.entry

Over the last few years, I have tried just about every RSS aggregator/reader out there—NetNewsWire, My Yahoo, RSS Bandit (written by Dare), NewsGator for Outlook, SharpReader, and so on. Each of them had something unique to offer...but for some reason, I just never got into the "groove" with any of them. A few days would go by, my number of unread entries would start to climb, and I would actually dread firing the app and changing all those bold entries back to normal. A number of times I didn't even read all the entries; I was just in a race to make myself believe I did before I went to bed.

Part of the problem for me is that applications that look and feel like Microsoft Outlook tend to make me feel like I am working, and I am immediately in "information overload" mode (we get hundreds of pieces of e-mail each day at Microsoft). Catching up with friends, reading Scripting.com, or checking out Engadget shouldn't be tedious. But for some reason, it was. Until I switched to Bloglines.

I had used Bloglines once for a couple of days but abandoned it because it didn't feel "rich" enough. It didn't have all the bells and whistles of NewsGator, and I mistakenly thought it would take me out of the task of opening Internet Explorer or Firefox to read messages when I could just as easily do it from within Outlook.

Now, sometimes with software (or anything, for that matter), you end up thinking you need more than you really do. And you commit to something—or purchase something—because of all the times you *might* need to use it, instead of all the times you *will* use it. That is how I felt when I bought every possible accessory for my Pocket PC, and that is how I felt before Bloglines. Everything that wasn't critical to reading feeds turned out to be inconsequential; I never used those features. The simplest solution is many times the right one.

Anyway, here is what I like about Bloglines:

- It's free.

- It's fast, responsive, and almost always available.

- Its design is minimalist and focused solely on the task at hand—reading RSS feeds.

- It is accessible from anywhere, so it works on my Mac, my PCs, and even my Audiovox Smartphone. Roaming read/unread status makes all the difference in the world.

- It supports sharing my feeds (check it out in the right-hand pane).

- I can scan dozens of feeds in less than a minute. With NewsGator for Outlook and other Outlook-style interfaces, it just simply took longer. This is probably because Bloglines shows me the feed in the way it is supposed to be presented—reverse chronological order on a single page, not as individual messages that I have to click through.

And here's what I want from it—if these things are already possible, please let me know:

- XMLHTTP to **precache unread items** as I am navigating down the list. Nine times out of ten, I am going to click the next bold link. It would be great if it was already waiting for me when I do. This isn't a huge concern, though, because it is normally snappy enough not to matter.

- Enhanced **keyboard shortcuts**. This is almost a must-have for me—I don't like switching from mouse mode to keyboard mode constantly. And given the option, I would rather be in keyboard mode than in mouse mode. At a minimum, providing a simple way to go to the next unread feed would be great. If this is already possible, I haven't figured it out.

- Easy **offline reading**. This is undoubtedly possible with Internet Explorer's offline mode, which just downloads the site itself, but does anyone actually use that feature? Even providing a button or a quick tutorial in the Help section on how to do this would be great.

- **Private feeds** (username/password). This is probably difficult for them with their cache as is, but it isn't really complete without it. I can't read Cassie's blog! (Cassie is a friend of mine in Ireland.)

This following is a blog entry from August 13th, 2005, on why I continue to use Bloglines:

STILL DIGGING BLOGLINES

Source: http://spaces.msn.com/members/mike/Blog/cns!1pG4qKNdtRA5Nl-UhvZl_1rQ!3334.entry

Back in December I posted about how much I love Bloglines in "Why I Dig Bloglines."

Well, here we are in August, and I still cruise over to Bloglines.com a few times each day to catch up on things. As much as I love Start.com, I just haven't yet been able to get into the same groove as I'm in right now with Bloglines. Blog-lines has 100 percent changed the way I use the Web, and that counts for something.

A year ago you would find me wasting 15 minutes a few times each day looking at a series of pages (my Favorites) that maybe changed every few days...and when I wasn't doing that, I was scanning My Yahoo every once in a while for new articles on things that interested me. What a complete waste of time that was! (Russell Beattie recently summed up the problem with portals like My Yahoo that treat all information the same way.)

Here is more on how I use Bloglines. Note that the things I dug about Bloglines in December still stand. In short, those things were *free, fast, minimalist, accessible anywhere, sharing, efficiency,* and *open APIs*.

- The **Bloglines toolbar button** to automatically subscribe to any Web page that has a corresponding feed. I use this three to four times a week.

- **Keep As New option** on posts. I use this all the time to keep something marked as "unread" until I am ready to clear it.

- **Newspaper view**. I click my feeds, and all unread posts appear on one huge page and mark all the posts as read. Because of this, there is no reason for me to spend the time categorizing my feeds into folders. Now, in a perfect world, the app would be smart enough to mark the posts read only if I scroll past them in the window...but that is probably wishful think-ing. I can scan hundreds of posts in no time this way.

- **Mobile version**. I also use this three to four times a week from my Treo 650. Of course, without roaming, my read/unread status would be pretty useless. But because I can get the same newspaper view on my mobile device, it makes all the difference.

- **Sort order**. Great feature. I have my feeds sorted by "# Unread," which is far more useful than scrolling up and down the page hunting for feeds in bold. I just found this option the other day, and I love it!

Bloglines has really opened my eyes to a few things as well:

- I've found that a bunch of the sites I used to visit daily I haven't visited in months. Why? Because they don't publish an RSS feed. It is just way too much work to manually check these sites when everything else comes to me in Bloglines. I would bet that more than **80 percent** of the time I spend "browsing" these days happens from within Bloglines. (Note to advertisers: this is **significant**!)

- I find things faster. I am exposed to 100 times as much information, and I spend far less time looking for it.

- The Web is ideally suited for an application like this. Roaming is inherent, so I never see the same post twice (with the caveat mentioned next). And I can get to the application from anywhere (work, home, my Mac, my Treo, and so on).

- As some of you may remember, Bloglines is a little messed up when it comes to feeds originating from MSN Spaces. Every once in a while you get a "phantom post" (sometimes it actually happens quite often), which makes reading spaces from within Bloglines pretty painful. We've let the Bloglines staff know about this, and we are working on a solution to this from our end as well.

So, there it is. **Bloglines is still my dawg**. But just like Virtual Earth did to my old Google Maps obsession, I don't expect it will be long before I am starting my day this way, especially with the pace those guys are keeping. I'll be impressed (but not necessarily surprised) if they can actually get me to switch.

(By the way, Bloglines calls everything a *feed* and always has, not an *RSS feed*—so much for that debate.)

Q: Do you have favorite feeds that you just *have* to read every day? What are they?

A: I really try to at least skim all my feeds once daily—but if I had to choose just ten, they would probably be these:

- CNET News.com (http://www.news.com)

- Scobleizer (http://scoble.weblogs.com)

- Russell Beattie Notebook (http://www.russellbeattie.com/notebook/)

- Engadget (http://www.engadget.com)

- Channel 9 videos (http://channel9.msdn.com)

- Superman Homepage (I am a big fan! http://www.supermanhomepage.com)

- WinSuperSite (http://www.winsupersite.com)

- Micro Persuasion (http://www.micropersuasion.com)

- Ed Bott's Windows Expertise (http://www.edbott.com/Weblog)

- Omar Shahine's blog (http://shahine.com/omar/)

Q: What kinds of feeds do you read? Name a couple that would surprise us.

A: I don't think any of the feeds I read are particularly surprising—I am pretty predictable in my RSS habits (although I do like to track celebrity sightings, but that's a topic for another day!). I read all sorts of stuff, but about 85 to 90 percent of what I read is technology related. I also read some sports feeds (go Yankees!), and of course, I subscribe to all of my friends' spaces.

You can actually check out most of the feeds I read on Bloglines (at least the ones I feel comfortable letting you know about!) at http://bloglines.com/public/mtorres.

Q: Do you have any pet peeves about RSS feeds?

A: A couple things bug me about RSS feeds today: 1) "partial content" feeds and 2) sites that support more than one feed to represent the same information.

- "Partial content" feeds are how some publishers hope to drive visitors back to their Web sites. Instead of including the complete item in the RSS feed, publishers include only the first couple of sentences or the first paragraph, and they ask users to visit the Web site to read the rest of the item. In my opinion, this makes RSS only "partially" useful. ☺

- Sites that support more than one feed are commonplace because of the different versions of RSS (and the existence of another syndication format called ATOM). Sites that support all these different formats are actually making it harder for their readers to subscribe to their RSS feeds, not easier. Asking the user to choose between version numbers when all they want is the actual content is crazy! It's almost like asking you which version of a Microsoft Word document you'd like to read when you click to open it, when all of the versions are the same except for some internal file format differences! Just offer your readers one syndication feed, and be done with it.

Now I think RSS as a format could handle a couple of things a little bit better, but one of the beauties of RSS is that it's extensible by the feed publishers. If RSS isn't suitable for whatever it is you're using it for, you can add your own functionality to RSS in the hopes that popular readers will support it. For example, Yahoo introduced Media RSS (http://search.yahoo.com/mrss) to make RSS a viable format for syndicating media content such as movies, images, and audio. Amazon has extended RSS to support its OpenSearch initiative (http://opensearch.a9.com), and Microsoft has extended RSS to help encapsulate lists of data where the order of the content matters (such as in wish lists or search results; see http://msdn.microsoft.com/windowsvista/building/rss/simplefeedextensions).

Other than that, my pet peeves are with existing RSS readers and not with the feeds themselves.

Q: Are RSS reads counted as site visits? Is there a downside to RSS (people never actually come to your space)?

A: Yes, RSS reads are counted in statistics as of September 2005. It's actually pretty difficult to accurately determine how and when people are reading MSN Spaces content via the RSS feed because each reader handles items a little bit differently. We just do what we can to make the best educated guess.

I don't see RSS as having a downside really. People will still visit your space because they like the way it looks or because they found it through your contact card or MSN Spaces Search. RSS is yet another way to make your voice heard!

Q: Is there anything else you'd like to tell us about RSS?

A: I love it!

Thanks, Mike, for sharing your excitement and vast experience with RSS and MSN Spaces! And...um...about that last answer? We already knew that! ☺

Advanced MSN Spaces—Undocumented!

APPENDIX B

Because MSN Spaces is so much fun—and because so many of you are quickly moving up into the ranks of "power users," we thought we'd invite Ryan Parsell, the guy behind the design of the MSN Spaces PowerToys, to add his perspective to the book. In the following interview, Ryan shares his views on these fun—and sometimes challenging—advanced features for your space.

Many of you are quickly moving up into the ranks of "power users."

PowerToys Interview with Ryan Parsell

Ryan Parsell is the development lead for the user interface team on MSN Spaces. He shares some insider knowledge about PowerToys:

Q: Are PowerToys dangerous? (Do they come with a surgeon general's warning?)

A: No, they're not dangerous, so to speak. However, they're risky to the point that you rely on them. You see, they're not guaranteed to work forever. Of the three that have been released to date, it's likely that two will be promoted to first-class parts and the third, the Tweak UI PowerToy, will be built into the product's customization settings. Once this happens, I don't know if we'll migrate users' settings from the old modules to the new features.

Additionally, if someone really tries, I bet they can wreck their space with these features. I think we've already taken care of a few of these bugs, but some of the customization features can mess things up if the person doesn't know what they're doing. This certainly isn't something that anyone using the Web page via the browser has to worry about.

The PowerToys are provided only in English. This isn't because we don't care about other languages and markets; it's just that I don't speak any other languages, and our localization team wasn't really let in on Power-Toys until it was too late. In fact, not many people outside the product team knew we were going to do this. That's the fun of it.

So, other examples of "danger areas" might be that in Tweak UI you can set your foreground text and background colors the same. This makes it rather hard to return to the PowerToy and reset the colors (because you can't see them!). Also, I think if you set some of the fields in your Windows Media Player part to wired decimal value, you get strange things. Unlike changing your screen resolution in Windows, the old settings will not revert after 15 seconds. The PowerToys were created with the involvement of the test team, but we set the bar rather high for the kinds of bugs we were going to spend time fixing.

Q: Where did the idea for PowerToys come from?

A: The Easter eggs [hidden, undocumented features] of a Microsoft that once was. ☺ Excel 5.0 had this egg in it. If you scrolled down to cell A95, entered this long block of text, and then opened the About Excel dialog box, you ended up in this little 3D maze room where you had to navigate to the end of the maze to see a wall with the names of all the contributors to that version of Excel. I told Jim Horne, our development manager at the time, that I'd love to do something like that in MSN Spaces. Now, this kind of thing has been taboo at Microsoft for years, at least in the Windows and Office divisions. (For obvious reasons, right? You can't show consumers, certainly not businesses and governments, that your product is secure if your developers have hidden code in it.)

Jim absolutely stunned me by agreeing that we should have some undocumented features in MSN Spaces. I even had people in my office when he said it. It was like he just said something incredibly obscene in front of a bunch a people and then walked out. I put it out of my mind for some weeks until after we shipped our v1 product. Then, out of the blue, one day Jim walked into my office, not speaking to anyone in particular, and stated aloud that he was "really disappointed that no one snuck anything into MSN Spaces." And turned and walked out. It was game-on after that.

Once the rumor started to spread in our product team, some people started calling them *Hacker Parts*. This really wasn't the case because by that time I had been quietly talking to a few people in our program management team about them. I also tried to recruit a tester to work some extra hours with me to ensure we met quality, performance, and security standards. But by that time our test manager had gotten wind of the project and had one of his test leads looking for any hint of these Hacker Parts. At that point, I had to come clean, and soon after, at a team meeting, I demo'ed seven PowerToys to the product team.

After some real project management work, some more development work, and some above-the-board testing, we had a few PowerToys that were beta worthy.

Q: What constitutes a PowerToy?

A: MSN Spaces was the blogging, photos, scrapbooking, and personal Web site for the masses. In the beginning, the hard-core bloggers were entrenched in other pay-for sites. Still others with more technical knowledge just hosted their own Web sites and domains. But as MSN Spaces has grown, it now offers some real value to these same hard-core content creators. The thing holding most of them back is the lack of customization and control over a space. This first wave of PowerToys is directed at those customers. PowerToys are accessible only by adding a little query string to the address bar. [Chapter 7 of this book describes that process.] If you don't know what a query string is, working with the most advanced PowerToy (Tweak UI) might be a bit much for you. Just take it slow, and ease into the "advanced" level.

PowerToys should do one of two things:

- Aid in advanced customization of a space
- Promote interaction between authors and visitors to a space

Q: Is there a secret handshake that goes along with it?

A: If I understand your question correctly, then I think Mike Torres must have tipped you off on this one. ☺

I so didn't want to post the keys (such as "&powertoy=sandbox") on any official sites. I wanted to leak keys out—one by one to our enthusiasts and a select group of our "day-one" bloggers—much more subtly than what ended up happening. I was ready to argue my case for this, but the way I remember it, our program managers had a sneaky little meeting while I was on a business trip, and I only had an intern in the room to defend my position. He did a good job, I'm sure, but needless to say I lost, and the Space Craft was born.

Q: As the creative genius behind PowerToys, what did you hope to accomplish with the MSN Spaces PowerToys? Are you pleased with the results?

A: OK, "genius" is going a bit too far. "Mastermind" works better for me. ☺

Really, at first it was to have fun creating small, useful modules and see whether we could get them shipped without all the red tape that usually goes along with releasing a feature. Then we started to see this as a good way to get customer feedback and to validate the MSN Spaces platform. We're now looking at the processes that facilitated their release to see whether we can use them to become more nimble in response to our customers' needs.

Q: Do you have a favorite PowerToy? What's so great about it?

A: Oh, I do. But it won't ship until after our next release in late November and then only if I can sell it to project management and management.

Q: How are MSN Spaces users using your PowerToys? Has anyone gotten really creative and used them in ways you didn't expect?

A: So, I ran the MSN Spaces booth at the product fair during the company meeting last week. We wanted to demo MSN Spaces as it was today, and we had some "slideware" showing what we'd have in our next version. It had been nearly a month since I just surfed around MSN Spaces using the Updated Spaces list. After a short time I found several sites doing all sorts of crazy things with PowerToys. One person had tried to rebuild what looked like MSN Spaces modules using the Custom HTML part with borders turned off and emulating the part HTML inside his Custom HTML...I don't know to what end. Many use the Custom HTML part to link to services that MSN Spaces has yet to provide intrinsically (for example, a public hit counter, affiliate advertising, Web instant messaging integration). This week we started looking at what percentage of people are using PowerToys, and we'll follow it up with, how are they using them? This is a great way to find out what areas we're deficient in. If someone has to take time to rewrite something that we thought we did a good job providing, we'd better take another look at our feature or at minimum the communication around how the feature works.

Q: Were there any PowerToy ideas that got left on the drawing board because they were too wild? If so, what were they?

A: I demo'ed seven PowerToys to the team during a meeting in the early summer. I convinced project management that five of them were worth the effort of writing mini-specs for testing purposes. In the end, we shipped three parts. One out of the five that dropped off the list was because of technical issues; more specifically, the framework that the part was built atop was not going to ship until the end of the year. Another part was scrapped because of a security concern; we had to give visitors write access to a field, and we couldn't be 100 percent sure in the limited amount of time we had that this wasn't going to open up a security hole somewhere in the product. I've since reviewed the concern and found it to be a nonissue, but at the time we obviously were happy to err on the side of caution.

There was a eighth PowerToy, coded for fun but too wild to ever be seriously considered. It was the Ouija board module. When two people were looking at the same space and one of them moved the Ouija pointer, the other person looking at the space would see it move too.

Q: Do you have a list of dream PowerToys that you'd like to see? Any chance they will be made available in future PowerToy rollouts?

A: Yes, and yes. ☺

OK, I've been avoiding the details of future PowerToys, not because I'm trying to be overly secretive. It's just that the list is volatile at the moment, and I'd hate to say I'm planning to do something specific, have someone get their hopes up (besides me, that is), and then not deliver.

One that I *will* disclose, which is *likely* to roll out in late winter, is Fridge Magnets. The author sets up a set of words, and anyone visiting the space can move them around to make sentences and save it so that all visitors and the author can view what was pieced together. Subsequently, any other visitor can take those words again and do the same thing—just like a set of fridge magnets. There are another six toys, and at least one of them is not a new module; it's something else altogether.

Q: Are there any stories, ideas, or suggestions you want to add for folks who want to get really good at using PowerToys?

A: Ah, just some advice. In the United States, people generally hate music to start when they visit a Web site, at least when it starts playing automatically. The

Windows Media Player PowerToy supports this, but if you like growing your audience, I'd suggest not doing it. This does seem to be a cultural thing, however. For example, in Korea they love music on Web pages. I'm not sure why this is.

Also, keep in mind that what's in a PowerToy today will likely be a fully supported feature in the future, so if the PowerToy doesn't offer everything you want, you can rest assured that we know it's a customer need and that we plan on addressing it formally down the road—except for Fridge Magnets, that is. I don't know *where* we'll go with that! ☺

INDEX

About the Authors

Katherine Murray has been writing books, articles, and Web content about technology since the late 1980s and during that time has seen a lot of change in the way we communicate and express

the stories of our lives. As a result, she's a major blogging enthusiast and actively publishes five blogs on various subjects. But she loves MSN Spaces best! Why? "You can do anything with it—write, share photos, communicate with friends, network, build an audience, and even add video and music! If there's another way you can think of to express yourself, it will probably be included in the next MSN Spaces release—if it's not in there already!"

Katherine has written extensively for Microsoft Press, focusing on topics related to Microsoft Office and digital lifestyle. You can find out more about Katherine's work at http://www.revisionsplus.com or visit her space at http://spaces.msn.com/livingspace.

Mike Torres is a lead program manager on the MSN Spaces team.

At Microsoft since 2003, Mike has worked with a variety of social computing services allowing

people to keep track of updates from friends and family and communicate with them on the Web or in real-time. Mike currently spends his days making various services such as MSN Spaces easier to use and more fun and helpful to an ever broadening audience of people.

Mike earned a bachelor's degree in psychology with a concentration in computer science from Cornell University and currently lives in Seattle, Washington with his wife Melinda. He also runs a popular weblog (blog) focused on MSN that has received nearly one million hits, making it one of the more popular MSN Spaces sites on the Web.

What do you think of this book?
We want to hear from you!

Do you have a few minutes to participate in a brief online survey? Microsoft is interested in hearing your feedback about this publication so that we can continually improve our books and learning resources for you.

To participate in our survey, please visit:
www.microsoft.com/learning/booksurvey

And enter this book's ISBN, 0-7356-2241-8. As a thank-you to survey participants in the United States and Canada, each month we'll randomly select five respondents to win one of five $100 gift certificates from a leading online merchant.* At the conclusion of the survey, you can enter the drawing by providing your e-mail address, which will be used for prize notification *only*.

Thanks in advance for your input. Your opinion counts!

Sincerely,

Microsoft Learning

Microsoft | Learning

Learn More. Go Further.

To see special offers on Microsoft Learning products for developers, IT professionals, and home and office users, visit: *www.microsoft.com/learning/booksurvey*

* No purchase necessary. Void where prohibited. Open only to residents of the 50 United States (includes District of Columbia) and Canada (void in Quebec). Sweepstakes ends 6/30/2006. For official rules, see: www.microsoft.com/learning/booksurvey